BORN CROOKED

The Forgers Whose Audacity Challenged the Pinkertons

For Roger and Nancy,
I hope you enjoy this tale of
rogues, rascals and Reformation.
It's a blessing to be re-connected
with you!

With love from your cousin,

Kim

12/11/17

Second Lock Press
Lancaster, PA

ISBN 13: 978-1-945028-10-6

For more information or bulk orders, please visit secondlockpress.com.

Book design by Adam Robinson for Good Book Developers.

BORN CROOKED

The Forgers Whose Audacity Challenged the Pinkertons

KIM Y. WITTEL

Second Lock Press

To Ivan

and

To the memory of my great-grandmother,
Fannie Lenox Shultz

CONTENTS

139 PART FOUR

173 APPENDIX

PREFACE

I⊤ WAS JUST a small article in a small-town paper.

A NOTED SWINDLER DEAD

Richard Lenox, a native of Mt. Joy, died in the Milwaukee house of correction, where he was serving a term for numerous swindling transactions he had engaged in in the West....Lenox was known to all the prominent detectives of the country, and when they did capture him he gave them a struggle to overpower him. He has spent half his life in jail.[1]

I had been researching my mother's ancestors off and on for some years, trying to discover what had happened to my great-great grandfather's family. My great-grandmother, who lived a long life and was full of stories about her own growing-up years, always said that her father never knew what happened to his four brothers and sisters. For some reason I was troubled by the thought, and began to investigate in my spare time. This was before the explosion of the internet and its amazing array of genealogical information, so I did a little bit here, a little bit there, and gradually pieced together the sad story of a civil war soldier who died far from home, leaving five small, orphaned children who were split up, never to be together again. As I worked to fill in the family story, I became aware that the soldier

---

1   Manheim [PA] *Sentinel*, "A Noted Swindler Dead." Nov. 10, 1899.

had a brother who also had disappeared. It was while I was working on something completely different that I ran across the article about Richard Lenox. I had a feeling I had found my man.

Not only had Lenox spent half his life in jail, he was associated with some of the most notorious forgers and confidence men of the nineteenth century, finally becoming a part of an infamous gang that operated all over the world and kept the famed Pinkerton Detective Agency going in circles in the 1890s. The story I uncovered is about these men: their methods, their technical brilliance and their amazing willingness to risk capture for the thrill of the challenge. But it's also about changes in the monetary and banking systems of the United States that came about because of the ease with which the men were able to work their schemes. And it's about William and Robert Pinkerton, the brothers whose name became synonymous with great detective work. The Agency founded by their father, Allan Pinkerton, changed the way policing and detective work was done in America. The Pinkerton Detective Agency was at the forefront of innovating how businesses formed alliances to fight crime, and in the age of rapidly changing communication capability, was the first nationwide crime-fighting force. The Pinkertons also helped to change the way our culture thought about criminal behavior, and how we addressed it. From the beginning, they focused on the rehabilitation of offenders after their debt was paid to society, and did everything they possibly could to help them re-integrate into the community. Their written communications with and about some of the principal characters in the story, which are found primarily in Part 4, are indicative of their concern for the men after their release from prison. It could be said that the Pinkerton brothers ran the original offender reentry program.

When I started my journey and discovered that the historical files of the Pinkerton Detective Agency were given to the Library of Congress in the year 2000, I thought that, perhaps, I might find something about Lenox and his life of crime. And I did! I found an incredible story full of colorful characters, backed up by a vast trove of Agency reports, newspaper articles from across the country, copious letters between Robert and William Pinkerton and to their agents in various places, and letters between the brothers and the men they tried to keep on the straight and narrow. The latter were of tremendous value to me as I sought to discover how these men operated, and why they went back, over and over again, to the life of crime that had such a hold on them.

Without the primary sources of letters and Agency reports, I would have had to rely on the journalism of the late nineteenth century. The sensationalist press was rampant, and even the best of newspapers often relied on whatever information they had, picking it up from another news outlet, until the story became an example of the "whisper down the lane" game. Hyperbole was common, and names, dates and details were often conflated to a degree that made any given article suspicious and certainly not a good source for the facts. But the newspaper articles usually pointed me in the right direction, and the Pinkerton Agency files provided the details and helped me verify the facts. I used only the fraction of the material in this vast collection that pertained to the story I wanted to tell. There are still many, many stories there to be found and told!

One of the things that is problematic in using nineteenth century sources is the lack of standardization of proper names. Not only did multiple journalistic sources spell an individual's name differently, but the name was often spelled several different ways within the same article. There were also different spellings of a name from primary document to primary document, and because the spelling of a name was simply not as important to people at the time, different branches of a family spelled their surname differently. Unless it is used in a direct quote, I have chosen to use the form of each person's name that was most often used in official documents, and that the person used most commonly in their lifetime. To reduce confusion for the reader, I have also not used any of the aliases that were employed by the characters in the telling of the story, again unless used in a direct quote. Each of them had aliases galore – some that they themselves used, some that were used by their partners, and some that were used by law enforcement. I have included a listing of common aliases that I found for the primary characters, although there were undoubtedly more.

That "noted swindler" that I set out to find led me to much more than I could have anticipated. The story I found was part of a much bigger story, one that captured my attention and imagination, as I hope it will capture yours.

"[Criminals] have all this essential moral beauty about them: they are all, in a real sense, reformers. They are all people trying to remove something from the fair face of life which prevents it being fully and naturally fair. They are all, I say, trying to remove something, if it be only a rich uncle. These criminals are all conditional optimists. Their action implies that they would be happy but for some removable obstacle; such, for instance, as the Chubb lock on a safe.

"Their quarrel with life is not essential. The thief says, 'If I could only obtain some more money (such as is at present temporarily in the possession of Mr. Miggs) how heartily I should fling myself into the sacred, the starry energy of the universe.'......These reformers use undesirable methods, and their conceptions of reform are commonly based upon a narrow and egotistic analysis of the malady of life. But they are reformers; they are not hopeless."

—*G. K. Chesterton*
Daily News, Dec. 30, 1905
Quoted in Gilbert Magazine, *v. 19, No. 4 p. 7*

INTRODUCTION

*I*N HIS BOOK, *POLICING THE URBAN UNDERWORLD: THE Impact of Crime on the Development of the American Police, 1800-1887*, David Johnson writes,

> Counterfeiting was probably the most lucrative, widespread, and complex crime in the early nineteenth century. It required considerable quantities of ink and paper, an engraver to make the plates, and some kind of printing press, but the absence of a national monetary system and the incredible profusion of local banks of issue provided counterfeiters with a wide variety of bills to copy and practically guaranteed them success....... Authorities discovered counterfeits only when they came to the bank of issue, or when they were so poorly made as to attract attention. [1]

Before the Civil War many, many dishonorable engravers and lithographers got away with counterfeiting State Bank bills and, eventually, US government money after the adoption of United States and National Bank currency. The fact that counterfeiting continued to be such a problem after the War led to the formation of a new law enforcement agency, the Secret Service. "With an estimated one-third to one-half of the currency in circulation being counterfeit, the Secret Service was commissioned on July 5, 1865, in Washington, D.C., as the 'Secret Service Division' of the Department of the Treasury and was originally tasked with the suppression

---

1   David R. Johnson, *Policing the Urban Underworld: The Impact of Crime on the Development of the American Police, 1800-1887* (Philadelphia: Temple University Press, 1979), 43-53

of counterfeiting."[2] The Secret Service was able to greatly reduce the counterfeiting of government money.

It was during this period in the late 1800s that "professional" forgers began to develop a well-thought out system of defrauding banks and other financial institutions in new ways.[3] Forgery at this time was "a complex procedure in which a variety of false instruments such as bank notes, drafts, bills of exchange, letters of credit, registered bonds, and post office money orders as well as checks were manufactured or altered and foisted off. … The technological characteristics of this kind of forgery made planning, timing, specialization, differentiation of roles, morale, and organization imperative."[4]

In an April, 1894, famed detective Robert Pinkerton wrote an article for the North American Review entitled "Forgery as a Profession," which laid out the process that was followed by nearly every gang that was operating.

Forgery gangs always consisted of people filling four different roles, which were sometimes combined:

1. *The Capitalist, or Backer*
2. *The actual Forger*
3. *The Middleman or Go-Between*
4. *The Presenter*

The Capitalist, or *Backer,* was the one who furnished the funds for the groups, usually laid out the plans for a job, and sometimes even procured the paper and other materials necessary for the actual forgery. The *Backer* rarely let himself be known to the *Forger* or the *Presenters.* He usually worked only with the *Middleman.* Occasionally, the *Middleman* and the *Backer* were one and the same. Being disconnected from the rest of the members provided protection from discovery if the people in the other roles were caught. He frequently

2   United States Secret Service. https://www.secretservice.gov/
3   *History of Henry Wade Wilkes.* Manuscript. 181-3 PNDA
4   Edwin M. Lemert, Charles C. Lemert, and Michael F. Winter, eds., *Crime and Deviance: Essays and Innovations of Edwin M. Lemert.* (Lanham, Md: Rowman & Littlefield, 2000), 98

wasn't even in the same city where the forgeries were committed. When a scheme was successful, the *Backer* received his outlay of funds back again, along with any funds that were "advanced" to make the plan work and, of course, a twenty to thirty percent cut of the "take."

The Forger was usually someone with knowledge of the printing profession, as well as artistic talent, and had a knowledge of chemicals that allowed him to alter checks, letters of credit and foreign currency so that the forgery was not easily spotted. He knew how to use paper pulp to fill up perforations in the original document or bill, and was able to restore the "delicate tints" in bank safety paper after the tints were destroyed by acid wash to erase the original information.

The Middleman, or *Go-Between* was a critical part of the team. Chosen by the *Backer* and *Forger*, he not only received the forged documents from the actual forger, but was charged with finding the *Presenter(s)* and accompanying him on the forgery job. He acted as the agent for the *Backer*, handing out funds for expenses and in general, managing the operations. He was, said Pinkerton, "usually selected for his firmness of character… a man known among criminals as a 'staunch' man, one who [could] not be easily frightened by detectives when arrested." He also had to have good relationships in the criminal world and, most important, had to have at least one record of criminal conviction against him. The latter item would insure that if the *Middleman* turned state's evidence, his record as an ex-convict would need to be strongly corroborated in order to be believed by the court. The *Middleman* usually picked out the bank to be swindled and found the appropriate presenters for the job.

The Presenters or *Layer-Downs* were chosen carefully by the *Middleman* and were always ex-convicts as well, to provide him with the same protection were they to give evidence against him. They were chosen from all ages and appearances so that they could successfully pass themselves off as porters, businessmen, stock traders or farmers, whatever was called for in any given situation. They needed to be believable in the roles they set up for themselves in a new town, as well as cool enough to pass the forged paper without attracting attention and leaving town without inviting suspicion. *Presenters* would usually victimize several banks in one location in a few hours' time to maximize the take from a particular town and leave before anyone had the opportunity to question them.

The division of the proceeds in a forgery gang was always agreed on beforehand. *Presenters* generally received from fifteen to twenty-five percent of small takes, and up to forty-five percent on larger ones, as they were more risky. The *Middleman* received fifteen to twenty-five percent, his responsibility being greater but his level of risk much less. The *Backer* and the *Forger* receive the balance, anywhere from fifty to sixty percent.

Usually, a certain amount of money was withheld from each successful job to be used in the defense of arrested members. Some gangs had an understanding that each man was on his own if arrested, although this was not appreciated by the *Presenters* who, after all, had the highest risk, and usually insisted on the system of "fall money" as protection. If a *Presenter* was caught or arrested, the *Middleman* immediately called off any other jobs in that town, and all members of the gang left town as quickly as possible, heading for a pre-determined rendezvous spot. The arrested man was provided with an attorney in return for the *Presenter* not confessing any knowledge of the rest of the gang. Told to plead guilty if a conviction looks likely, the Presenter trusted the attorney's promise of working to get him a short sentence, but was often disappointed when he was abandoned by the gang.

The actual forgery of a document was usually done in one of three ways: by raising or altering bank drafts, by forging signatures or endorsements of depositors or payees, or by gaining the confidence of a bank or company official who could provide actual blank drafts or checks. As Pinkerton explained it in an 1886 *New York Times* interview,

A deposit of a respectable amount was made in some bank, which was made the basis for obtaining a letter of credit, certificate of deposit, or certified check. From a bankers' directory or some similar source the gang obtained a list of the banks with which the bank that had given them the letter of credit corresponded. Duplicate forms of the bank's business paper, certificates of deposit, and official seal were manufactured. Filling in these blanks with amounts to suit themselves, the forgers wrote letters of introduction to the banks they intended operating on, purporting to introduce the party holding the letter of credit, who would soon call on them, and requesting for him the usual accommodation. Some of the letters contained what was said to be a genuine signature of the man holding the letter of credit, and gave a partial description of the person whom it was intended should pass the forged paper. All being in readiness, the genuine letter of credit would then be taken to the point where the swindlers had represented to the bank of deposit that they intended to use the money, and where they had been properly introduced by genuine official letters. After the money had been obtained from the bank on the genuine letter of credit one of the gang would return to the town from which the letter had been obtained and by an understanding with his confederates would begin mailing the forged letters of introduction in facsimile envelopes of the bank, containing a signature of the party to whom they had made the forged letters of credit payable, and sending the forged letters to such banks as had been agreed upon. An understanding was arrived at between the leader and his confederates as to the date and the exact time the letters of credit were to be presented, and it was arranged to have the forged letters of introduction reach their destination one day before the forged letters of credit were presented at the bank designated. In presenting the forged letter of credit the swindler would give urgent reasons for wishing to use a large amount of money at once. Should the bank decline to cash the paper until it had telegraphed to the bank purporting to issue the letter of credit, the swindler would pleasantly acquiesce and promise to return the next day. He never returned.[5]

---

5 *New York Times*, "Ready For Jail Again," Jan 22, 1886. http://nyti.ms/2vIQGpC

What follows is the story of Charlie Becker, along with a loosely woven gang of thieves and forgers, who for decades kept law enforcement busy on both sides of the Atlantic. It was during the second half of his criminal career that Charlie and a small group of confederates managed to confound the newly emerging Pinkerton Detective Agency, prompting changes in the monetary and banking systems of the United States. Before they were finally brought down by the Pinkertons, this gang was considered "the most clever combination of bank swindlers of modern days," and was thought to have swindled banks in the United States out of more than $1,500,000 during the time they worked together.[6] They dropped and added other confederates as they went along, abandoning and selling them out as needed, but by the 1890s, Charlie Becker, Richard Lenox, and Robert Bowman had become the principals of the most prolific forgery ring of the nineteenth century.

6　*The Pioneer Press*, "'Big Dick' In the Toils." July 13, 1894. 77-5 PNDA

PART ONE

"Criminals, among each other, have standing and tone, precisely as do members of society.... A brilliant raid upon a bank, an extraordinary swindle in Wall Street....a fine piece of check-raising, or a handsomely-made counterfeit bond, Government note or bank-bill, are each accomplishments, in their line, to be proud of, and to cause as much praise and envy as the most laudable success can compel in commercial, social or literary circles."

—*Allan Pinkerton,* Professional Thieves and the Detective *(p.69)*

"Want is not the sole incentive to crime," wrote Aristotle; "men also wish to enjoy themselves and not to be in a state of desire – they wish to cure some desire, going beyond the necessities of life, which preys upon them...and therefore they commit crimes."

—*Arthur M. Schlesinger, Jr., quoted in* Thomas Byrnes' Professional Criminals of America *(p.xiii)*

SOME NEFARIOUS WORK

O N MAY 2, 1859, A GERMAN EMIGRANT NAMED CLE-
mens Hering opened an account at the New York Emigrant Savings Bank. The Bank was established in 1850
by members of the Irish Emigrant Society and served thousands of
Irish emigrants, as well as emigrants from other countries. Clemens was from Baden-Wurttemberg in Germany, and was part of the
first wave of German immigration to America. Most of these new-
ly-arrived Germans settled in an area called "Kleindeutschland," on
what is now Manhattan's Lower East Side, and their industriousness
reflected the culture they came from, with its long history of the
guild tradition and its emphasis on achieving the highest possible
rank in their chosen trade.[1] By 1855, New York City had the third
largest population of Germans of any city in the world, and a thriv-
ing German-American community.

Hering recorded that he arrived in the United States sometime
in 1836. His family consisted of his wife, Barbara Rembler (some
sources say Kennler) Hering, and three children – two sons and a
daughter. The 1857 New York City Directory shows Hering living
on Frankford Street, and making his living as a printer. In 1865 the
family was living in Orangetown, Rockland County, and by the time
of the 1870 census, Clemens, Barbara and now their five children,
including their eldest daughter Anna, 15 years of age, were living
back in Manhattan on Broome Street, where Clemens continued to
list his profession as "printer."

---

1   Richard Haberstroh, *Kleindeutchland: Little Germany in the Lower East
Side.* Lower East Side Preservation Initiative, http://www.lespi-nyc.org/

Hering *was* a printer – more accurately a lithographer – but by this time, he and Barbara had begun using their skills in a new way to support their growing family. As early as June of 1862 they were caught passing counterfeit quarters. When they were arrested, police searched their residence and also found a lithographic stone used for printing Confederate $20 notes, as well as stones for making notes on Virginia and North Carolina Banks.[2] By 1870, Clement, as he was now known, had discovered the way to keep one step ahead of the law. Known to be "a dangerous associate for young Germans," he had a reputation, especially for drawing young waiters and bartenders into assisting him by passing his counterfeited money. "He enticed them by stories of the riches to be made," said the New York Sun, "and when they got into trouble he deserted them." [3] Indeed, when he was arrested in a printing establishment near Beekman Street on a charge of counterfeiting Internal Revenue Bank check stamps, he quickly turned state's evidence against his co-conspirators, receiving a pardon for being the "principal witness" in the trial of another counterfeiter charged with making plates for counterfeiting currency. [4] On July 24, 1871, Hering enlarged his family when Anna married John Charles Becker, known as Charlie, one of the "young Germans" he had enticed to join him in his "trade."[5] Now sixteen, Anna was an attractive young woman with a light complexion, light brown hair and lovely light blue eyes.[6]

John Charles Becker was born on July 7, 1848, in Minden

2   *New York Daily Tribune*, "Counterfeiters Arrested – Confederate Lithographs in Their Possession." June 11, 1862. http://bit.ly/2x4uINt/
3   *New York Sun,* "Tracing the Big Forgery." April 20, 1877 http://bit.ly/2i61CL6
4   *NYS*, "Closing In Upon Forgers." April 11, 1877 http://bit.ly/2wfiLYe
5   New York, New York City Marriage Records, 1829-1940," database, FamilySearch http://bit.ly/2uICpfB 20 March 2015, John Becker and Anna Hering, 24 Jul 1871; citing Marriage, Manhattan, New York, New York, United States, New York City Municipal Archives, New York; FHL microfilm 1,544,495.
6   Report, [1896?], Container 78 - Folder 4, Pinkerton National Detective Agency Records

m'Hannover, to John C. and Wilhelmini Borgemer Becker.[7] He immigrated to the United States as a young man, where he learned engraving as a trade, and was quite adept at it. He soon found himself courted by the members of a particular segment of the underworld for his potential as a counterfeiter, and through his father-in-law Charlie Becker fell in with a notorious gang of thieves and forgers led by "The Napoleon of Crime," Adam Worth. For Charlie, it was the start of a life-time career.

*   *   *

It was in July…when a well-dressed man entered the banking house of John S. Gittings & Co., at North and Fayette streets [sic], and said he wanted to rent an office on the first floor of the building on South Street, near Lombard, adjoining the old third National Bank site. The property was owned by the Gittings, and the man, who said his name was Stabler, soon closed the deal for the rental, paying $650 for the first six months of a year's rent. He said he was the senior member of the firm of Stabler & Co., grain commission men, and the firm had decided to locate in Baltimore, which city offered many advantages to a firm in his line of business.

The next day a wagon-load of furniture backed up to the office adjoining the Third National Bank, and the office was soon furnished. Conspicuous among the things taken into the Stabler & Co. office was a large map. Those who saw it afterward remarked that it was hung on the north wall of the Stabler office, which wall was next to that of the Third National Bank. [8]

Sometime on Sunday, the 18th of August, 1872, The 3rd National Bank of Baltimore was robbed of over $200,000 cash and securities, mostly those of the B&O and Northern Central Railroads. Three of

7   New York, New York City Marriage Records, 1829-1940," database, FamilySearch (http://bit.ly/2i4LYiW : 20 March 2015), citing Marriage, Manhattan, New York, New York, United States, New York City Municipal Archives New York; FHL microfilm 1,544,495

8   Manuscript, from Clinton McCabe, *History of the Baltimore Police Department 1774-1907*. 77-1 PNDA

the four safes in the bank vault had been broken into and emptied of their contents and the Baltimore Police Department could see pretty quickly that the bank vault had been smashed into from the back, through the common wall with the office of Stabler & Co, where the large map of the United States covered the hole. Timbers, jackscrews, iron bars and other burglars' tools were found in the Stabler office as well, but there was no sign of "Mr. Stabler."[9] Neighbors reported that "a light would frequently be visible at late hours in the officers of the 'Grain merchants,' but as they were extremely affable gentlemen, who were always ready with a good cigar and a cheery word to the policeman on the beat, no attention was paid to the late business hours they maintained." At 3:00 a.m. on the morning of the crime, two policemen had even seen them walking down the street carrying suitcases. The officers "had exchanged a cheery good morning with the two men, who had offered them cigars which the policemen refused, being on duty."[10] The thieves' plan was ingenious:

> Operations were commenced by breaking away a portion of the wall in the "Stablers'" rear office at a point just opposite the position of the bank vaults. The opening began at about three feet from the floor and was four feet square. This work must have all been done upon successive days or nights for several weeks, and between whiles the damage to the wall was hidden by the use of a large cotton sheet… [with] mucilage or gum on the edges and there were corresponding marks on the wall, showing where it had been hung. But not relying upon this safeguard, a map of the United States was made to serve also in the same nefarious work…. The hole commenced in the plaster of the "Stablers'" inner office, continued through six courses of brick, which was in itself no mean undertaking, and required good tools as well as patience, and having accomplished this the operators were encountered by the iron rear wall of the vault….The inside of the iron vault was lined with several courses of brick. Within there was still an iron door to be forced and boxes or

9   NYT, "Heavy Bank Robbery," Aug 20, 1872, http://nyti.ms/2fLB0hv
10   Exhibition Text, "Burglary of the Third National Bank of Baltimore, Md." 34-9 PNDA

drawers to be ransacked....Having with such address, courage and cunning secured the booty which the bank guardians supposed to be so securely protected, [they] left the premises. [11]

At first, Baltimore police were stumped in their efforts to apprehend the thieves and recoup their losses. That is, until bank officials contacted the Pinkerton Detective Agency for help.

*   *   *

URBAN POLICE, AND police detectives, in the mid-1800s, were often suspect in the minds of the populace, and sometimes for good reason. Timothy J. Gilfoyle, in *A Pickpocket's Tale,* tells how "at the lowest level, police officers on the street routinely tolerated certain amounts of crime such as pickpocketing, as long as they received a percentage of the loot, hence the label 'percentage copper.'....Detectives represented another layer of corruption.... [A New York] state assembly investigation in 1875 concluded that precinct detectives literally managed financial relationships between captains and the 'criminal classes' in their precinct. In effect the detective was a reverse confidence man, someone who employed illegal methods in the name of the law, turning crime fighting into a system of blackmail."[12]

By the mid-1840s, "the constable-detective was believed to be closely linked with the criminal classes as a 'go-between.'"[13] So it was no surprise that a new type of "private policeman" began to emerge across the country. Former police officers, retired or politically "on the outs," were some of the earliest of this new profession, sometimes

11   Jacob Frey, *Reminiscences of Baltimore.* (Baltimore: Maryland Book Concern, 1893), 241-243. http://bit.ly/2wavs7q

12   Timothy J. Gilfoyle, *A Pickpocket's Tale* (New York: Norton, 2006), 247.

13   Frank Morn, *The Eye That Never Sleeps: A History of the Pinkerton National Detective Agency* (Bloomington: Indiana University Press, 1982), 13.

called "Independent Police."[14] In the early 1850s, "a slightly different individual emerged – entrepreneurs who had either minimal police experience, or none at all….Allan Pinkerton…was the most successful and probably the most efficient of this new type…"[15]

"'The Eye,' as Allan Pinkerton was called, was well known to the members of the nineteenth-century underworld. They knew he was incorruptible and so was his agency. They were also well acquainted with Pinkerton's tenacity; if necessary he would chase you to the end of the earth."[16]

Allan Pinkerton was born in Glasgow, Scotland on August 25, 1819, the son of a sergeant in the Glasgow Police Force. He and his new bride immigrated to Canada in 1842, and eventually on to northern Illinois, where he established himself as a cooper, the trade in which he had been employed in Scotland. He also became heavily involved in the abolitionist movement, and his home and cooper shop in Dundee, Illinois were well known places of safety for escaped slaves making their way north. In the mid-1840s, Pinkerton was cutting wood for his barrels on an island in the Fox River when he stumbled on the headquarters of a gang of counterfeiters. What happened next, changed the course of his life and the lives of his sons, as well as the nature of crime-fighting in the United States. He and the local sheriff managed to arrest the men, after which he became somewhat of a local celebrity and was convinced by town merchants to help end the "fast-growing problem of distribution of fake currency."[17] Pinkerton, in his book, *Professional Thieves and the Detective*, related that "the country being new, and great sensations scarce, the affair was in everybody's mouth, and I suddenly found myself called upon,

---

14   David R. Johnson, *Policing the Urban Underworld* (Philadelphia: Temple University Press, 1979), 59-60.

15   Ibid.

16   James D. Horan, *Desperate Men: Revelations from the Sealed Pinkerton Files*(Garden City, NY: Doubleday and Co., 1962)

17   Riffenburgh, Beau, *Pinkerton's Great Detective* (New York: Penguin, 2013), 17

from every quarter, to undertake matters requiring the detective skill, until I was soon actually forced to relinquish the honorable though not over-profitable occupation of a cooper, for that of a professional detective."[18]

He was made deputy sheriff for Kane County, and soon held the same position in Chicago's Cook County. By 1850 he had been named to Chicago's new police force as its first "detective."[19] But within the year, he had resigned his position to form his own detective agency for the Chicago area, where he was hired by the Chicago post office, as well as the railroads, investigating everything from counterfeiting to kidnapping. By 1860, his firm had officially become Pinkerton's National Detective Agency, the first and most well-known private detective agency in the world.

The Pinkerton Agency quickly earned a national reputation, and expanded to include offices in New York (opened in November 1865) and Philadelphia (opened in May 1866), along with the home office in Chicago, solving some of the biggest crimes of the day. Their unremitting pursuit of legendary criminals like Jesse James, Butch Cassidy, and the Dalton Brothers made them the foremost crime fighting resource, and the go-to agency for police departments across the country. Pinkerton and his agents, which he called operatives (he called himself the "principal"), worked undercover, providing some of the earliest covert surveillance for major railroads, the Chicago Post Office, and the United States Army, routing out corruption, interrogating deserters, and uncovering black-market racketeers.[20] With the motto, "We Never Sleep," and the famous unblinking eye logo, the term "private eye" was born.

Since corrupt behavior among law enforcement was at that time an expectation of many citizens, it was important to Pinkerton to combat this reputation, and he instituted a strict code of conduct,

---

18   Morn, 21.

19   Allan Pinkerton, *Professional Thieves and the Detective*. New York: Dillingham, 1900 http://bit.ly/2hY4edM, 16

20   Riffenburgh, 19-20

published in 1878 as the Pinkerton Agency's *General Principles*, which made clear that agents were required to behave with the highest sense of honor, and always to treat criminals justly and fairly. The "pernicious practice" of accepting rewards for services rendered was strictly forbidden. A Detective was expected to be "impartial in all his operations, and to guard himself against prejudice on the one hand, and favor on the other....He must credit neither good nor ill of any man, upon hearsay...No man ought to be made to suffer on suspicion only."[21] In fact, Pinkerton's concern for the well-being and reform of the criminal was as original as some of his methods, and helped change the direction of the criminal justice system to include rehabilitation along with punishment. Unlike New York City's famous police chief and detective Thomas J. Byrnes, who believed that reformation of "professional criminals" was impossible, Pinkerton felt very strongly that "[t]he criminal must not be hunted and persecuted after he has paid his debt to society, but helped to become an honest and reputable character."[22] This concern for the soul of the offender played a large part in the sometimes symbiotic relationship that often developed between detective and criminal. "As a rule these men are not ungrateful," said Robert Pinkerton in a letter to the Centennial Meeting of the Pennsylvania Prison Society. "I have seen cases in which reform has been accomplished, and some instances of failure in the attempt; but I have yet the first case to see wherein the criminal was so ungrateful as to turn his hand and do an injury to his benefactor."[23]

After suffering a stroke in 1869, Pinkerton continued to direct the agency, and the investigations, from his office, but most of the

21   *Transactions of the Third National Prison Reform Congress Held at St. Louis, Missouri, May 13-16, 1874.* New York: Office of the Association, 1874. http://bit.ly/2uVdXD3, 245-246

22   Horan, 59.

23   *The Journal of Prison Discipline and Philanthropy,* "Report of the Commemoration of the 100th Anniversary of the Pennsylvania Prison Society." no. 26, January 1887, Philadelphia: The Royal Printing Company http://bit.ly/2uVdXD3

field work was taken over by his two sons, William and Robert. He also published over a dozen books of detective literature. The genre of the detective story had gained huge popularity after Edgar Alan Poe's stories were published in the 1840s, and the industry of "pulp literature" and police gazettes with sensational stories made them even more so. William and Robert Pinkerton, along with what was by now hundreds of agents, were using new and original methods for both detecting crime and capturing perpetrators. By creating the "Rogue's Gallery" of criminal photographic portraits and detailed accounts of each criminal's habits, associates and "haunts," the Pinkerton Agency laid much of the groundwork for the entire profession for decades to come.

* * *

IN THE BALTIMORE bank robbery job, the Pinkerton detectives suspected members of the loosely-formed gang that surrounded "The Napoleon of Crime," Adam Worth.

Most sources say that Adam Worth was born in Germany around 1844 and immigrated to America with his parents at the age of 5. According to William Pinkerton, Worth developed a taste for swindling early on and was said to have effected multiple desertions from the Union Army during the Civil War, always re-enlisting under a new name to get the bounty, and then repeating the process. When he settled in New York after the war, he quickly fell into the crowded underworld of the City, acquiring the nickname "Little Adam," partly due to his short stature, and continued his criminal career by picking pockets and petty thievery. When he managed to escape from Sing Sing Prison in 1865, after only a few weeks imprisonment, his reputation rose among his peers, and they began to take their marching orders from him. Between 1866 and 1870 Worth "was the brains of a gang of professional robbers who levied generously upon banks and business houses."[24] The Pinkerton Agency did its best to keep ongoing tabs on the members of Worth's gang, but because members were always circling in and out it was difficult, if not impossible, to be aware of all their activities. The Agency, though, quickly determined that two of its members, Joseph "Little Joe" Elliott and Charles Becker, among others, were responsible for the Baltimore robbery.

Probably born in the early 1850s, Elliott was much younger than many of the others in Worth's orbit, but still had a good start on his criminal career. Described by a Baltimore police officer in his recollections of Baltimore crime annals, Elliott had been "a shoplifter, an associate of criminals, a sneak thief and finally a master of the art of 'doing the unwary,' so that he always seemed to have a pocket full of money… He could dress, drink, talk and play well; what more could be desired?"[25] "An inoffensive-looking little man,"[26] Elliott was first arrested in Philadelphia in the 1860s for pick-pocketing. He served time in Philadelphia's Moyamensing Prison and by 1870 had moved on to New York where he "got in good" with the members of Worth's set. Descriptions of the elder and younger Stabler in the Baltimore robbery corresponded with Becker and Elliott, respectively. One account reported that both Stablers "dressed handsomely, kept large bank accounts, and soon became known in the neighborhood as good fellows, free with their money and evidently doing a good business." [27] Becker, who was just beginning to establish his reputation among the criminal element as well as with law enforcement, one day asked a cashier at the bank to show him how their firm's considerable money was kept safe. The cashier was only too happy to give the elder "Mr. Stabler" a tour of the vault, assuring him that it

---

24   Richard Wilmer Rowan, *The Pinkertons: A Detective Dynasty.* (Boston: Little, Brown, and Company, 1931), 273.

25   Frey, 245

26   Thomas Byrnes, *Professional Criminals of America.* New York: Cassel & Company, 1886, 73

27   *San Francisco Bulletin*, "Charles Becker, Prince of Forgers." Sept 28, 1903. 77-7 PNDA

old, 5 feet 6 inches, stout and corpulent. Elliott was noticeable for being "very small…clean shaved, excepting [a] slight moustache."[2] Sometime around the 24th, Chapman bought goods from a local tailor and asked about a good bank in which to deposit a sizable amount of money.[3]

By September 28 Chapman's wife, Lydia, had arrived in Liverpool, having sailed for London on the SS *Cuba* on the 18th.[4] Chapman left London to meet her ship, returning on September 30. On October 5, William Pinkerton arrived in London and began shadowing the three men, as well as others of their group who had also sailed from the United States in September. The eldest of Allan Pinkerton's sons, William, born in 1846, was the principal of the Chicago office. Thought to have been kept in Chicago under his father's eye because of his "outgoing jovial life-style" and excessive drinking,[5] William was oriented to field work, keeping tabs on miscreants and forging the symbiotic relationships with criminals that made the work of the Pinkertons so successful.[6] His brother Robert, born in 1848, controlled the New York and Philadelphia offices and was more administratively oriented. He had studied business at the University Of Notre Dame, and personified the role of "detective as administrator."[7]

By the time William arrived in London, Chapman had rented a home at 103 Neville Road where he was joined by Lydia on October 17. Soon Elliott and Becker rented rooms at 24 King Henry's Walk, where Chapman visited the two almost daily. The three men were also seen meeting with others of the criminal persuasion who were known to the Pinkertons, including Max Shinburn, Ike Marsh, and

---

2 George H. Bangs to AP, Jan 5, 1873. Letter. 76-6, PNDA
3 George H. Bangs to WAP, Dec 28, 1872. Letter. 76-6, PNDA
4 Ibid.
5 Morn, 91.
6 Morn, 129.
7 Ibid.

"Bottle Sam" Perry at one of the two homes, or at a local watering hole called "The Fox Hound."

In early November, Chapman somehow managed to disappear from surveillance, although it was later discovered that a T.J. Wilson had opened an account at the Provincial bank in London in favor of a "Lydia Wilson," from which Lydia Chapman withdrew £220 on November 12. Chapman's movements were of particular interest to the Pinkertons. He was suspected in an earlier forgery in the U.S. and while the detectives were still trying to gather the evidence to charge Becker and Elliott with the Baltimore bank robbery, they knew that Chapman had been involved in the forgery case. Because burglary was not an extraditable crime in Britain, but forgery was, they felt sure that Chapman had not been aware that extradition papers had been prepared for his forgery crime, and that he felt secure in staying visible in England with Becker and Elliott.

On the other side of the Atlantic, Pinkerton principals were watching closely the travels back and forth between Europe and the United States of many of the men's confederates, and enlisting the help of several informants in trying to make a definite case against Becker and Elliott for the Baltimore robbery. Bank officials had given the Pinkertons latitude to continue the investigation overseas for at least two more months, but decided that they couldn't afford to continue it beyond that. They would, they said, be willing to "forego the benefit of another dividend if they could get the parties and con-vict them," but several of them felt it would be a useless expense, and that "the parties were too smart" for them.[8] Robert Pinkerton confirmed with his father that the underworld scuttlebutt was that Mrs. Chapman had slipped her Pinkerton shadow after arriving in Liverpool, but that she and her husband were again "picked up" in London. Chapman had somehow gotten wind that the extradition papers on him were for the forgery crime, so he had gone under-ground. On December 1, William Pinkerton arrived in Paris, where

---

8   George H. Bangs to AP, Dec 12, 1872. Letter. 182-6, PNDA

he received a telegram from his father saying, "Willie we must win. Never give up." He showed up at Adam Worth's American Bar, causing some moments of concern, but Worth relaxed when he learned from an informant the Pinkerton was only on the trail of the Baltimore thieves.[9]

By January, all the minor players in the Worth circle had returned to New York City, while Becker, Chapman and Elliott remained in Europe. When there was a hint of Chapman being spotted in Brussels, William Pinkerton received the word from his father to go there looking for Chapman and, if found, to "arrange a shadow there and capture him when he left."[10] George Bangs, general superintendent of the Pinkerton Agency's New York office, wrote William on January 10 and affirmed the plan to continue with the surveillance, wherever it took them. "You have had a very uphill road," he said, "and have worked away at it with more courage and determination than what anyone could have expected, but notwithstanding the untoward circumstance I feel certain that if the Bank will continue to back us you will yet be able to carry the matter to a success."[11] Pinkerton informants in the U.S. continued to work their sources for information on the bank robbery, but got nowhere. Mrs. Chapman was reportedly "putting down a new carpet" and making household purchases, which suggested the she, and perhaps the others, were in for a long stay.

---

9   RAP to AP, Dec 16, 1872. Letter. 76-6, PNDA
10   George H. Bangs to AP, Jan 9, 1873. Letter. 76-6, PNDA
11   George H. Bangs to WAP, Jan 10, 1873. Letter. 76-6 PNDA

THE ROPE WAS READY

ECKER, ELLIOTT AND THE CHAPMANS LAID LOW during the next few months. No records have been found to show that any of them were suspected of or captured in any crime, and while local law enforcement continued to keep them under surveillance, William Pinkerton returned to his home base in Chicago early in 1873.

But the men were busy. Sometime during 1874 forged letters of credit began to show up in banks throughout Europe, most of them drawn on London's Bischoffschiem, Goldsmith & Co., Baring Brothers, or the City Bank of London. As was typical in this segment of the underworld, the three enlisted the help of other members of the gang who were available in Europe at the time. They posed as wealthy travelers and got away with quite a few successful gambits. In Frankfurt-am-Main some of their group was apprehended, but the rest escaped and split up, to ply their trade in Austria and Belgium, while Becker, Elliott and Chapman made their way to the city of Smyrna, in Turkey.

When the three arrived in Smyrna in 1874, they had been operating successfully, so far, in every place they tried. But local law enforcement caught up with them there where they were arrested, tried in a British Consular Court and convicted of forgery. They were each sentenced to three and a half years in a Consular prison. According to an 1886 interview with Becker, the prison "hadn't anything but mud walls, and we'd have left it quick enough if we'd cared to. It was the country, not the jail, that held us. We couldn't get out of the country."[1]

The local officials must have known that the Smyrna prison was inadequate to hold onto the experienced thieves they had locked up, because after a few months they were transferred to an Engxlish prison in Constantinople to serve out their sentences, one with "walls four feet in thickness, solid cell doors and cast steel grate-bars an inch and a half square."[2] In the Constantinople prison, the three met up with another of the Adam Worth's gang members who had been arrested in that city for passing forged notes on the Ottoman Bank, Carlos Siscovitch.

Carlos Siscovitch, sometimes known as Charles or Ivan, was born Carlos Grandi of an Italian father. As her children carried Siscovitch as their middle name and Carlo was often called "the Russian," their mother may have had Russian roots. Their father was a barber in Washington D.C., and at some point after his death there, their mother moved the family to the Los Angeles, California area where at least three of her four sons became masters in the world of criminal forgery. Louis Grandi, alias George Siscovitch died in Folsom Prison in 1889 for check raising. Henry, a law student in the office of a San Jose judge, forged the judge's signature and disappeared on the East Coast in the early 1880s with $3000.[3] Carlos was born in the late 1840s and by 1870 had made his way to New York City where he mingled easily with the thievery and forgery crowd, eventually owning a saloon under the Edwin Booth Theatre at 60 W. 23rd Street, which became a notorious hangout for the local underworld.[4]

In an effusive letter to his wife Alima, dated January 29 1875 and using the alias "Howard Adams", Siscovitch claimed to have arrived in Turkey on October 8 or 9 with the forged letters of credit.

---

1   Brooklyn Eagle, "Little Elliott." March 20, 1886 http://bit.ly/2uIReP6=

2   Ibid.

3   I.W. Lees to WAP, Dec 30, 1889. Letter. 76-7 PNDA

4   Byrnes, 325

On the 12th he tried to draw fourteen hundred pounds sterling at a local bank, but raised enough suspicion that he was arrested while breakfasting at his hotel the next morning. He handed the ill-gotten money over to the officials and was arrested by Turkish police. He was put in Turkish prison in Constantinople where he was "left to rott[sic]…for over fifty days." He claimed to have nothing given to him to eat except bread once a day, no bed to sleep on, and was "packed to the number of thirty five or forty in a room not large enough for twenty." [5]

After a Turkish trial, with no witnesses, jury or legal defense, Siscovitch was sentenced to a Turkish Convict Prison, although shortly was transferred to an Engxlish Prison, where he met up with Becker, Chapman and Elliott. In an 1886 prison interview, Becker spoke openly about what happened next.

As Becker told it:

> We got tired of [the] seclusion. It took almost a month before we could fix things… The cell doors locked with top and bottom bolts, and though each had its key there was a general key that fitted all of them. A key like that was useful and it was by a mere accident that we got one. It happened one day that the prison marshal…came rushing in to have a prisoner sign some papers, and rushed out again, leaving his key sticking in the keyhole. It wasn't very long before we had an impression of it, and it was back in the lock again. After getting the shape of the key we had Mrs. Siscovitch bring us two blank keys, some little files, Turkish caps and three lanterns. About midnight…we went out and steered at once for the storeroom where our clothes were piled away. We broke open the storeroom, got our things and then found our way into the yard and sized up the prison wall. It was forty-two feet high but…our rope was ready. [It] was weighted with a piece of wood and we threw it over the wall to catch it at the grating and by fastening it there were able to climb to the top. We escaped and met a friend, who took us to his home where we

5   Carlos Siscovitch to Alima Siscovitch, Jan 29, 1875. Letter. 76-6, PNDA

stayed for two months. I sent Elliott to England after some money I
had there, and when it came we went to London also. [6]

Going back to London, though, was a problem. When Becker,
Elliott and Siscovitch escaped the Constantinople prison, they left
Joseph Chapman behind. Said Becker, "there was good reason for
it. He gave us away three times and as we wanted to get out we
did not include him in the fourth attempt." [7] Since their home base
in London was Joe and Lydia Chapman's house on Neville Road,
they needed to make amends with Lydia. While en route to London,
Elliott had to pawn his gold teeth for ready cash, but when they
arrived at Neville Rd. they expected to claim their share of the money
they had been sending back to her during their European spree.

Becker and Elliott arranged to board with Lydia, while Siscovitch and his wife said they were going back to America. Lydia Chapman, at the instruction of her husband, "persistently refused to give
up any part of the money" that the thieves claimed as theirs.[8] While
the conspirators were concocting their next move, Lydia Chapman
wrote to an old colleague of her husband's by the name of Charles
Pontez in New York. Complaining of the ingratitude of Becker and
the others, she asked Pontez to contact Wilkes for his help in freeing
Joe.[9] By this time, Siscovitch and his wife, who had not returned to
America, and who Becker did not like or trust, showed up at the
Neville Road home. After Wilkes refused to help in freeing Chap-
man, Becker and Elliott departed from the Chapman home, leaving
Siscovitch and his wife there.

Two months later news came that Lydia Chapman was found
dead in her home, and the Siscovitches had disappeared. Becker
always thought that her death was the result of a plan by the Siscovitch pair to rob Lydia that went horribly wrong. Thinking that

---

6   BE, "Little Elliott." March 30, 1886

7   Ibid.

8   NYT, "Check Raisers Caught." May 14, 1896 http://nyti.
ms/2fZAVHl

9   Ibid.

their rightful share of the money was somewhere in the house, so the story went, on April 13, 1876 they drugged her liquor and planned to search the house until the money was found. But instead of the few hours of unconsciousness they expected, Lydia died. A jury later ruled that she might have died of an underlying heart problem, but the suspicion that the couple was responsible for her death never entirely disappeared.

*   *   *

IT WASN'T UNTIL twenty-three years later, in early January of 1899 when William Pinkerton received a letter from Adam Worth that the real story of the Constantinople episode was revealed.

According to Worth, it was he who sprang Becker, Elliott and Siscovitch from the Turkish prison in 1875. The men had indeed been operating under his auspices, but he… "experienced the disability attaching to all genuine 'master minds' of the underworld," and had to endure the slip-ups and treachery of those under him who were not to be trusted.[10] When he learned of the men's capture, he traveled to Constantinople and spent a fortune on bribery and arrangements to obtain their release because, according to the Pinkertons and his own criminal contemporaries, he "never forsook a friend or accomplice."[11] Although his plans seemed at the time to have failed, the men later assumed that it was Worth's money that induced the guard to "accidently" leave the key in the keyhole so that they could make their escape. Worth, however, was beginning to tire of Becker, who he said was "the biggest coward in the world," and decided to have no more to do with him. Although he had made a good deal of money with him over the years, Becker's tendency to "squeal" made him more of a liability than an asset.[12]

---

10   Rowan, 274

11   Pinkerton's National Detective Agency, *Adam Worth, Alias "Little Adam"* (New York: Feb 1903), Preface http://bit.ly/2uPI5QM

12   RAP to WAP, Jan 16, 1899, Letter. 182-6 PNDA

THE $64,000 QUESTION

A SMALL ARTICLE IN THE JANUARY 18, 1877 NEW YORK Times announced that "it was rumored on Wall street early yesterday morning that 'a great forgery' had been detected, and that the Union Trust Company had been victimized for a large amount."[1] The paper reported that the following had been sent out over the wires at the request of Mr. King, the President of Union Trust:

> The public are cautioned against negotiating our check, No. 10,392 for $9,500, gold, on Bank of New York, certified by bank, payment having been stopped on account of fraud.[2]

But the amount of the fraud was much, much greater - $64,225, to be exact. As the story unfolded over the course of the next three months the police, and the public, heard a tale of deception, revenge and intricate scheming that went much deeper than they had first imagined.

As reported by the Times, on January 2 a check was presented to the cashier of the Union Trust Bank for $64,225. The check bore the signatures of Morris Franklin and William Beers, President and Actuary of the New York Life Insurance Company, respectively. The insurance company had a long-standing account with the Bank, which was located at the corner of Broadway and Rector Streets. The signatures looked genuine, as usual, and the cashier certified the check without any hesitation.

---

1   NYT, "A Large Forgery." Jan 18, 1877
2   Ibid.

That same day Mr. G. L. Maxwell, a broker with an office on
nearby New Street, reported that he was approached by a man who
called himself Mr. Brown. The man was "dressed fashionably, had
pleasant manners, was good looking and had an agreeable way of
talking."[3] Brown, Maxwell said, presented him with a letter signed by
a Mr. Franklin of New York Life, in which Mr. Maxwell was asked to
"state the terms upon which he would act as the broker in Wall Street
of the Insurance Company," the Company being unhappy with its
current broker.[4] Maxwell asked for time to think about the matter
and the next day, January 3, Mr. Brown showed up at Maxwell's
office with the check for $64,000, certified the previous day. When
Brown asked him to purchase $50,000 in gold for him, Maxwell and
a colleague agreed. They delivered the gold and deposited the check
in the Mechanics' Bank, after which it was honored by Union Trust.

"Mr. Brown," it was discovered much later, was actually Joe
Elliott. When Elliott and Charles Becker returned to the United
States after escaping from the Turkish prison in the summer of 1876,
they lost no time in planning their next swindle. According to testimony in their trials later that year, they ran into each other on
8th Avenue in August or September and planned the Union Trust
job over the course of the next few months. A few days after the
November 7th presidential election, Elliott brought to Becker a cancelled New York Life Insurance check and asked if he could copy it.
Problems with matching exactly the paper and ink took Becker some
time, but finally, the week before Christmas, they met in their friend
Siscovitch's saloon under Booth's Theater and planned the final
details. On January 1, 1877, Elliott appeared at Becker's house and
told him to get a check ready for the next morning – the job was a go.

When the accounts of the New York Life Insurance Company
with the Union Trust Bank were audited on January 10, the cashier
of the insurance company was stunned to discover the $64,000

---

3   George W. Walling, *Recollections of a New York Chief of Police* (New
York: Caxton Book Concern, 1887), 340 http://bit.ly/2waFCoo
4   Ibid.

check of which he had no recollection, and which was not recorded in the checkbook. The check itself looked completely genuine, and he took it to President Morris Franklin who was just as astonished and knew at once that it was a forgery, despite the amazing facsimile of his signature. Franklin immediately contacted officials at the Union Trust and Mechanics' Banks. The first public mention of the affair was in the January 18th Times article warning the public of the rumored fraud. In the days leading up to the announcement, several possible suspects were questioned and arrested. Unwilling to believe that none of those involved in the chain of transactions had fuller knowledge than they claimed, the District Attorney ordered the arrest of Horace E. Browne (not the "Mr. Brown" who had originally approached Maxwell), a broker who tried to sell one of the gold checks, as well as G.L. Maxwell, the broker who initially purchased the gold for Elliott on the $64,000 check, and George Chadwick, who purportedly told Browne about a company, New York Life, that wanted to get depreciated securities in "an indirect way," and initially approached Browne about the scheme. All three admitted to their involvement, but all three denied any knowledge that the $64,000 check was a forgery.[5]

According to Maxwell, he had met Horace Browne for the first time the previous October. Shortly before Christmas, Browne approached him about buying gold and securities for "an institution that wanted to do a good deal of business on the street."[6] He agreed to do so and secretly divide the commissions with Browne and someone inside the institution, which Browne now revealed to him as the New York Life Insurance Company. In fact, said Maxwell, he told Browne that he was going to have the check certified, to which Browne agreed.

How the scheme worked, said Horace Browne during his trial testimony, was that 55% of the commission would go to the company, 20% to the officers of the company and 25% to Maxwell and his friends. Browne then testified that Maxwell told him he had consulted a lawyer and had been told that he couldn't be held criminally liable, since the check would be certified by the Trust Company itself. On January 2, when Elliott, as "Mr. Brown," appeared in Maxwell's office with the New York Life check, the conspirators followed through with purchasing the gold certificates as planned, with no suspicion that the check from New York Life Insurance was fraudulent.

On March 29, 1877, Horace Browne and George Chadwick were indicted for forgery in the third degree, while the case against Maxwell was dismissed. Although the specifics of the various transactions that had taken place since January 2nd were testified to in court and reported daily, in detail, by the newspapers, authorities remained tight-lipped about their investigation; but they had their suspicions. As one unnamed detective said, "It's not a fresh hand that shaped this business, nor was it the work of a hitherto square man. If it was we should believe the offender had fled. A 'cross' man, or an old hand at forgery, would stand still and take events quietly."[7]

On Wednesday, April 11, the New York Sun reported that Clement Hering, John Worth (brother of Adam Worth), Charles Becker and his wife, Anna had been arrested the previous day in connection with the Union Trust forgery case, although the District Attorney said the case "had not been sufficiently developed to warrant publicity being given to the facts."[8] The police also refused to give details, but admitted that the long-time family of forgers were involved. They did say that the three men were arrested based on evidence that would shortly be made public. Becker's wife (Hering's daughter) was held "to prevent her from communicating with other members of the gang" but was quickly released.

Elliott was arrested as well, and he and Worth were arraigned

---

7   NYT, "The Great Forgery." Jan 19, 1877 http://nyti.ms/2waRQx8
8   NYS, "Closing In Upon Forgers." April 11, 1877 http://bit.ly/2wfiLYe

on the 13th. Worth was discharged for lack of sufficient evidence and Elliott's case was adjourned until the following Monday. On Monday afternoon, Elliott was brought before Justice Kilbreth at the Tombs, the popular name for New York's Hall of Justice and "America's greatest criminal barracks," and formally charged with "having assisted in the forgery and utterance of [the] $64,000 check upon the Union Trust Company, purporting to have been drawn on the New York Life Insurance Company."[9] Becker and Hering were also charged at the same time.

The Tuesday morning newspapers told quite a tale about how the authorities managed to tie Hering, Elliott and Becker to the Union Trust business. It seemed that one Augustus Sohn, a truck driver, had been apprehended on the morning of February 20th with a truck full of goods stolen from T.B. Pettie & Co. of Chambers Street. He quickly fingered his accomplice, John Peters and also promised that if he were relieved of charges in the theft, he would give the police information that would help them apprehend a gang of skilled forgers.

When his offer was accepted, Sohn told them that several days prior he had been employed by Clement Hering, whom he had known for some fifteen years, to move furniture and other household items from 402 E. Twelfth Street to 30 Amity Street. Among the items he moved were a large "machine," later identified as a printing press and waxed stones from which impressions of checks or bonds had been taken. This was enough to give the authorities grounds to arrest Hering and the others on suspicion of being involved. According to the New York Times, Hering and Becker were already under suspicion, since they had begun to "purchase large quantities of household articles, and also made overtures for the purchase of real estate" shortly after the $64,000 check was negotiated the past January.[10]

At Becker and Elliot's arraignment hearing, Mr. Beers of the New

9   NYT, "The Union Trust Forgery." April 17, 1877 http://nyti. ms/2fKYoMc
10   NYT, "The Great Union Trust Forgery." April 24, 1877 http://nyti.

York Life Insurance Company spoke at length, and affirmed that the check in question was clearly a forgery, that the paper that was used was slightly different that the company's normal checks, and that he had never signed it – although, he said, his signature was so well imitated that it must have been traced. That day's witnesses included the Union Trust bank teller who certified the check and Horace Browne, who repeated the story he had previously given the police with the additional identification of Elliott as the "Mr. Brown" he saw on January 2nd who brought the check to Maxwell. When Browne was asked if he recognized the prisoner Becker, he said he "might" have seen him in Chadwick's office, but was not sure. He again swore that he had no knowledge of the check being a forgery, and pointed out that he immediately went to authorities with the story of his and Maxwell's scheme when questions first arose about its genuineness.

When court resumed on Tuesday, George Maxwell also identified Elliott as the bearer of the check on January 2, but emphatically denied Browne's testimony regarding his part of the scheme. When Augustus Sohn took the stand, he spoke of moving the lithographic materials for Hering and Becker several times and testified that one of the times he moved them recently, Becker promised to buy him a horse if he said nothing about it. Becker, he said, told him they were doing something "quite large" and would soon have "big money."[11] Hering told him, he said, that they were making a check or a bond, and when he saw the account of the $64,000 forgery in the newspapers he asked Hering about it. He said he then complained about the smallness of the sum that was given to him and Hering said "Becker was a mean man" and asked him to say nothing about the affair. He also told him that $30,000 of the proceeds went to "a man downtown" who "stood in with the party."[12] When accused by the defense of self-serving motives in coming forward, Sohn admitted his motives

ms/2x4VCF4

11   NYT, "Union Trust Forgery." April 18, 1877 http://nyti.
ms/2w1XXU0

12   Ibid.

evidence, and when Phelps took the compelling evidence he had to Elliott, in the Ludlow Street Jail, Joe agreed to tell all he knew.

After he purchased the gold through Maxwell on the forged check on January 4th, said Elliott, he and Becker met to split the wealth. But it wasn't split just among the forgers. There was, indeed, an "inside" man who procured the cancelled check and eased the way for Becker and Elliott, and he was none other than Charles Pontez, the go-tween that Lydia Chapman had contacted from England in an effort to get money from George Wilkes, so that her husband could be freed from the Turkish Prison.

Charles Pontez first made the acquaintance of Joseph Chapman in 1866, when he was a clerk employed by the Union Navigation Company, where Chapman was Secretary. He left the Union Navigation Company after a few years and in 1869 was hired as a policy clerk by the New York Life Insurance Company. Through Chapman, Pontez met Becker, Elliott and other members of the counterfeiters' underworld, and was drawn into the plot they hatched to defraud the bank. It was easy for him to procure cancelled checks from the office as samples and return them to their rightful place a few days later. He was always aware, as well, of the amount that New York Life had on deposit with the Union Trust Bank, and so knew the most opportune time for the swindle.

A few days after the deed was accomplished, Elliott, Becker and Pontez met in a barber shop where Pontez told Becker to speak quietly as there was "some trouble about the affair in the office..."[2] Becker and Elliott knew then that the forgery was in danger of being discovered, and stayed out of contact with Pontez from that point on.

By the time he approached Elliott for corroboration, D.A. Phelps had been suspicious of Pontez for some time. After Lydia Chapman's death in England in 1876, Pontez' s letter in response to her plea for financial help to get her husband out of prison was found

2   NYT, "The Union Trust Forgery." Nov 20, 1878 http://nyti. ms/2fKQbrl

among her effects, proving his relationship to members of the gang. It was then discovered that Pontez had served as Joe Elliott's best man when he married on August 31, 1876 at the "Little Church Around the Corner." When Pontez resigned his position with New York Life in mid-October, Phelps knew he had to move quickly.

It was announced that Becker would be tried in a few days and Pontez was sent for as a witness in order not to tip him off to the authorities' suspicions. On Wednesday, October 23rd, 1878, the Grand Jury indicted Charles Pontez for forgery and he was arrested at the house of friends on West Fourteenth Street. He was arraigned and, of course, plead not guilty. Although his attorney appealed to the court to set a low bail since his client was charged with only "an ordinary case of forgery," the prosecution said that, on the contrary, Mr. Pontez had associated with "the most daring and expert forgers in the country," who had pulled off "the forgery *par excellence* in the history of crime in this country."[3] Unable to make his $20,000 bail, Pontez was committed to the Tombs.

The trial for Pontez began on November 18. Pontez himself barely spoke, but had his lengthy affidavit read by his counsel. In it, he insisted that he was innocent of the crime he was charged with, and that he had no idea what kind of testimony may have been brought forward against him. With the large number of conspirators involved, and the "large number of detectives employed at large wages to convict somebody," he feared that he would be made a scapegoat.[4] When the prosecution began, one of the critical pieces of evidence was the introduction of a cancelled New York Life check in the amount of $150,000 that could be proven to be the check from which the forgers traced the signatures of Beers and Franklin. As Robert Pinkerton later revealed, the forged check was placed over the cancelled checks in the insurance company's vault one by one until the correct check was discovered. Not only were the signature strokes

---

3　NYT, "The $64,000 Forgery." October 25, 1878

4　NYT, "The Union Trust Forgery Case." Nov 19, 1878 http://nyti. ms/2i5Igpl

corresponding but the signatures' distance from each other as well. At that point they knew this was the check that had been furnished to the forgers by an employee of the company.

The prosecution also relied heavily on the testimony of Charles Becker that he and Elliott had met Pontez some years before through his relationship with Chapman. They saw him again in London at Chapman's home. When they returned to New York after their escape from Turkey's Smyrna prison in July of 1876, they met him on 8th Avenue, and then several times after that. According to Becker, the three of them devised the plan. The Times reported the detailed description given by Becker of the preparations.

> A few days after the election of 1876 [the conspirators] had a meeting and Elliott then handed the witness a canceled check of the New York Life Insurance Company, and asked him whether he could engrave checks like it; the check had been for $200,000; it was rejected because a hole had been punched through the vignette; it was handed back by Elliott to Pontez, and a few days afterward the latter brought a canceled check for $150,000; the witness took that and made a lithograph engraving of it, and printed a facsimile from the stone; when Pontez saw the copy he said it looked very well indeed, but that the print was too blue; the witness took it away and made the desired alteration...[5]

There was then a delay until Pontez confirmed that there was enough money on deposit for the check to go through easily. Just before Christmas Becker testified that Pontez gave him a piece of paper with the "running number" of the check. Elliott showed up at Becker's home on January 1 and the plan went into action. The signatures on the forged letters, explained Becker, were traced freehand, while the signatures on the check were traced with a brush since more care was needed.

Becker testified that on January 4th he and Elliott met with Pontez to divide some of the proceeds, and again on January 12th or 13th

---

5   NYT, "The Union Trust Forgery." Nov 20,1878

in the barber shop, corroborating Elliott's story. Finally, he said, he had met up with Pontez some eight or nine weeks ago in a street car and the latter had "winked at him not to recognize him." [6]

When the defense opened the next day, Pontez's attorney pointed out that Pontez had never attempted to leave the country, or even the City during the twenty-one months since the forgery, a strong suggestion of his innocence. When Pontez himself took the stand, he denied all involvement with the crime. He did admit traveling to Europe in 1874 at the behest of Mrs. Chapman, but said he had no recollection of meeting either Elliott or Becker at that time. He had met Elliott a few years prior, through Chapman, and yes, he had served as a witness to Elliott's marriage in 1876, but only because he had just run into him and Elliott needed a witness on the spot. When his letter to Lydia Chapman was produced, he admitted writing it, but claimed not to remember the exact context. When he wrote that "he was grieved because certain parties failed to stand by Chapman to the last," he said, he didn't know that those parties were Elliott and Becker.[7]

The case went to the jury on November 21, 1878, after a lengthy summation by the prosecution and detailed instructions by the judge. After three hours the jury was unable to agree on a verdict and was sequestered until the next morning. When the court was called back into session the judge asked if they had reached a verdict. "We could not come to an agreement," said the foreman, "if we should remain out a month." [8] Standing solidly six for acquittal and six for conviction, the jury was dismissed, and Pontez, suffering from tuberculosis, was released on bail. By the time his second trial was called in December he was unable to appear and physicians sent to inspect him reported that he was dying. On February 7, 1879, Pontez died

---

6   Ibid.

7   NYT, "Charles Pontez On Trial." Nov 21, 1878 http://nyti.ms/2vE2NWL

8   NYT, "The Pontez Jury Disagree." Nov 23, 1878 http://nyti.ms/2v1WQz9

Wilkes had been busy since he and Becker last worked together. Since an 1870 arrest and dismissal of charges, he had traveled the country, and the globe, perpetrating fraudulent schemes by himself or with others, and had managed to stay just out of the grasp of the authorities. He and Joe Chapman had worked their trade in St. Joseph, Missouri, Council Bluffs, Iowa and Cheyenne, Wyoming. From there they headed to San Francisco, then to Acapulco, Mexico and Panama, hoping to buy some time in case the law was close behind. In late 1871 Wilkes returned to the United States briefly, then went to Havana, Cuba to meet up with Chapman as they earlier had planned. Soon after, they headed for New England, where they defrauded a bank in Connecticut, followed by trips to Chicago and Louisville, Kentucky for the same. Thinking that they should lay low for a while, they returned to New York City and spent the next few months planning "a new operation."

In early 1880, Wilkes headed to England, where he welcomed the arrival of Charlie Becker, George Engels, Shell Hamilton, and several other minor members of the forgery community to London in June, including Bill Bartlett, Peter Burns, Henry (or Edward) Cleary, Henry Wilson and George Bell. Wilkes and Engels, who was notorious for his involvement in the Bank of England forgeries in 1873, had a plan to flood Europe with forged drafts and forged letters of credit by taking "five different directions on the Continent and [defrauding] all the bankers they met in their way." [4] They began by sending men to Toulon, Brussels, Rotterdam, Amsterdam, Berlin, Hamburg and Bremen, with instructions to assume the role of American tourists, and "to procure drafts from bankers on their correspondents in London." [5] But by then, Wilkes and Engels had learned that New York's Inspector Thomas Byrnes had contacted the London police with the names of all the gang's members, so the plan was abandoned, at least for the time being. Since they had yet to

---

4   Byrnes, 304
5   Ibid.

engage in anything criminal and couldn't be forced to give evidence as to what the gang was planning, some of the less important members of the group were sent back the America, while Engels, Wilkes, Becker and Hamilton stayed in London.

Becker and Engels soon began working on forging Italian bonds while they were staying in a house on Leamington Road with Wilkes and Hamilton. Small denomination Italian bonds, which had been brought back by the earlier scouts, were erased by the two expert forgers, and the paper was restored to its original color. Then new figures were printed on the notes with a plate made by Becker. The group managed to dispose of the raised bonds with the French Credit Lyonnais, the Parisian Bank, the Societé Generale, and the Caisse Generale of Paris, netting 400,000 francs which they neatly divided among themselves. They continued their thievery throughout the next few months with the assistance of like-minded criminals in France, Belgium and Italy, while Engels and Becker forged everything from banknotes to letters of credit to passports.

In early December Becker and Engels, who were being watched closely by law enforcement on both sides of the Atlantic, returned to the United States, hoping to throw off suspicion, while Wilkes and Burns continued to work with their Italian network. Waiting until Becker and Engels had safely landed in New York, in order to confuse the police, Wilkes began testing the forged notes, but in Florence, the law caught up to him and he and Burns were arrested there on Christmas Day. The arrest was immediately telegraphed by the Consulate to the authorities in New York, where they were urged to arrest Becker and Engels, whose involvement was easily recognized through communications picked up between the two of them and Wilkes.

Engels was arrested on December 31, 1880, and taken to police headquarters, but Becker apparently knew he was under surveillance, as he was observed leaving his home on the 29th, and had not returned. Detectives were stationed outside the Beckers' Cypress Hills house, where they watched for Becker's return from behind a nearby fence. Finally, at 2:00 a.m. on January 1ˢᵗ, 1881, Charlie was spotted entering the house, and was quickly apprehended and transported to police headquarters to join Engels. United States Consul General, Schuyler Crosby was notified in Italy of the arrests by Inspector Byrnes, and received word by return telegram that the Italian government planned to send the necessary extradition papers promptly. Both men were taken to court for arraignment on January 3, while law enforcement waited for the Italian government to make their expected case for extradition.

But Becker's string of good fortune was about to be extended again. On January 5ᵗʰ, both Becker and Engels were released from custody by Commissioner Osborn after three appearances before him on a petition by the Italian ambassador in Washington for their commitment to jail, while awaiting the approval from President Rutherford B. Hayes for extradition. The problem was that by even their third appearance before the Commissioner, there was "not a line or particle of evidence of any sort" that was presented.[6] On January 4ᵗʰ, their attorneys moved for Becker's and Engels' discharge on four grounds, the most pertinent being that the Court, under the treaty of extraditions between the US and Italy, had not acquired jurisdiction of the prisoners. As reported by the Times:

> The fifth subdivision of the treaty of extradition with Italy required, in direct terms, that the first step in a proceeding for extradition should be the presentation by the petitioning Power of a **duly-authenticated copy of the record of conviction, or of the warrant issued against the person** [emphasis mine] sought to be extradited; that such certificate should be first presented to the President of the United States, and that then he should issue his mandate to the judicial authority for the issue of a warrant for the arrest of the accused person.[7]

---

6   NYT, "A Treaty With a Hole In It." Jan 6, 1881 http://nyti.ms/2v01G4Q

7   Ibid.

Although not a common clause in most extradition treaties, the Commissioner did find it in effect with several countries, including Italy, the conditions of which "tended to embarrass the operations of justice…" [8] So the prisoners, having been imprisoned for a mere few days, were discharged.

*   *   *

WILKES' ARREST IN Florence on December 25, 1880, proved to be the beginning of the end for the long-time criminal who was once known as one of the most successful of crooks in the country. In order to save himself, and knowing that Becker and Engels had escaped conviction, Wilkes made a remarkable confession to Consul General Crosby, not only of his most recent crimes, but of his entire criminal life to that point. And he didn't shy away from implicating all his confederates' involvements, either. Although criminals often embellish confessions to heighten their own importance and feed their own egos, New York's Detective Inspector Byrnes, when he read the transcript of Wilkes' revelations, was "satisfied that every word of it was true…"[9]

Notwithstanding his confession, Wilkes and Burns were put on trial, but Wilkes's attorney was able to secure his release on the grounds that "his confession having been made to the American Consul General instead of an Italian official, was invalid for purposes of evidence."[10] Burns, along with a few of his other comrades, was put in prison and Wilkes returned to the United States where he lived off his ill-gotten gains for the next few years.

*   *   *

---

8   Ibid.
9   Typescript of *New York Herald*, "King of Forgers was George Wilkes." April 4, 1897 181-6 PNDA
10   Ibid.

By 1885, WILKES had run through all his savings, and was *persona non grata* among many of his old criminal pals for implicating them in his confession. Then he ran into Little Joe Elliott, who had been released from prison in 1881, after spending three years in prison for the Union Trust forgery. By the summer of 1885, he and Wilkes, along with Joseph Chapman, had put together a band of forgers and began a spree which took them throughout the western United States and Canada, until they were apprehended in March, 1886, for a forgery in Rochester, New York. Captured in New York City, they had left a trail of forgeries behind them in Wyoming, Montana, Oregon and California before making their way to Rochester in August, where they made away with $4,500 from forged checks on the Banque du Peuple of Montreal.[11]

Pinkerton detectives had been one step behind the men most of the way, but couldn't get the drop on them until finally, they learned through an informant that the men were holed up at the home of a confederate on 125th Street, near 8th Avenue in New York City. They were kept under surveillance until an opportune time, and the detectives, along with New York City police, picked them up on March 18, 1886. Wilkes and Elliott were taken back to Rochester where on the 12th of May, Elliott was sentenced to 15 years in prison. He was granted a pardon in 1892 by New York's Governor Flower, "obtained through the intercession of a prominent US Treasury official," but died in a New York hospital in December 1893, of typhoid fever. [12]

Remarkably, Wilkes escaped conviction, but he quickly ran through the proceeds from the recent forgeries and the few friends he had left quickly tired of him asking them for loans. This once notorious forger, who had "possessed a distinguished manner, was a brilliant linguist and conversationalist, and always prided himself on his personal appearance," began to drink heavily, begging on the street

11   NYT, "Two Forgers Arrested." March 18, 1886 http://nyti.ms/2v1rWXY
12   Thomas Byrnes, *Professional Criminals of America: New and Revised Edition* (New York: G.W. Dillinham, 1895), 51 http://bit.ly/2wPJN61

in ragged clothes and being evicted from even the lowest saloons and hotels.

Finally, on the night of April 7, 1892, a New York City patrolman found what he assumed was a tramp lying unconscious in a vacant lot at 38th Street and 10th Avenue. Badly beaten and left for dead, the officer took him to Bellevue Hospital where it was discovered that he was the infamous forger. He died there on April 14, 1892, "penniless and friendless." [13]

---

13   History of Henry Wade Wilkes, Alias George Wade Wilkes, Expert Forger. Manuscript. 181-3, PNDA

THE FAMILY BIBLE

T HE HEADLINE IN THE SEPTEMBER 17, 1881 *NEW YORK Times* read, "A Noted Counterfeiter Arrested after Long and Patient Watching." Charlie Becker had been under scrutiny by the authorities ever since his release from custody in January, when the Italian government was unsuccessful in its attempts to extradite him for the European bond forgery. Ostensibly, he had retired to the country with his family, his father-in-law Clement Hering in tow, and rented a home in an "isolated place in the suburbs of East New York."[1] The home, "with a cupola, in a lonely neighborhood," was situated so as to give them an excellent view all the way around, which gave the police heightened suspicions.[2] While it is unclear at what point Becker and his family began being shadowed, testimony in his trial made it clear that as early as June, authorities had a suspicion that Charlie was up to his old tricks.

When on June 17, Mr. James Walsh, a banker and broker on Wall Street, sold a 1,000 franc Banc of France note worth $192.50 to an unidentified customer, Becker was already under surveillance by a private detective firm operated by James Mooney and John Boland. They were, they said employed to watch Becker and Hering by "persons desiring to have cases worked up," against them.[3] Although the detective firm never revealed how and when the surveillance of Becker was begun, they were clear on one point: information had

---

1   NYT, "A Noted Counterfeiter Arrested After Long and Patient Watching." Sept 17, 1881 http://nyti.ms/2vDdQPQ

2   BE, "Is it Becker?" May 29, 1888 http://bit.ly/2wPSOMx

3   BE, "The Alleged Counterfeiter on Trial for Forgery." Nov 29, 1881 http://bit.ly/2w1PEaZ

been given to them that connected the legitimate June purchase of the Banc of France note with clandestine activities that were taking place in the Brooklyn home of Becker and Hering. Some thought that Joe Elliott "squealed" on Becker for turning state's evidence in the Union Trust job. Others surmised that Frank Hering, Becker's brother-in-law who also lived in the Brooklyn house, gave him up when Becker slighted him in the planning of the job. In any case, the story of how Mooney and Boland managed to insinuate themselves into the life of the family and thus get the advantage on them on the night of September 16th, 1881, is a story that shows to what lengths the authorities were willing to go to "get their man."

After the note sold by Walsh made its way to Becker, he and Hering, with the cooperation of Anna and the others in the house, began to amass the materials needed to create forged Banc of France notes of high quality – the only kind that would satisfy Becker's standards. Once Mooney and Boland were tipped to the plan, they contacted both Coudert Brothers, who served as counsel for the French government in the United States, as well as the Banc of France. Coudert Brothers asked Mooney and Boland to investigate thoroughly on behalf of the bank.

Their first step was to rent an adjoining house to Becker's and have a "family" move in to operate a boarding house. The boarders, of course, were undercover detectives. From that point on Becker's home was watched day and night by one of the operatives, and note was made of every person that went in or out of the house. Anyone who left the house was shadowed to their destination and back, and anyone who was met by the suspects was also suspect. One of the "boarders" soon made friends with a servant girl at Becker's home and became her "cousin," giving him open access to the house. Although the Becker household seemed suspicious of the boarding house at first, they soon let down their guard and the neighbors were visiting each other in the yard, but never invited into the house. As they began to feel more comfortable with their new friends, Becker and his family couldn't resist talking about their "project," and bragging

the water mark of the paper of the note, several proofs of the note which had been struck off on glazed paper, and several thousand sheets stamped with the water mark and thoroughly prepared for the press, and four presses on which the printing was to have been done."[8] The notes themselves were said to be so well-crafted, that even the president of the Banc of France could not tell the counterfeit note from the genuine one.[9]

Becker asked for an adjournment until he had secured counsel, and both men were held over for trial. They were brought back to court on the 21st, adjourned again, and held over for the Grand Jury.

*   *   *

THE TRIAL FOR Becker and Marks finally began on November 28, 1881. Prosecutors however, quickly entered a *nolle prosequi* (do not prosecute) in the case of Nathan Marks, so that he could testify as a witness against Becker. Becker was indicted for forgery in the second-degree, on fifteen counts. Detective Mooney described in detail the circumstances of his firm's surveillance of Becker on behalf of the Bank of France, as well as the particulars of his arrest. Mooney itemized the materials found in Becker's laboratory, including engraving tools, the lithographic stone, gelatine papers, printing presses, acids, inks, and a great quantity of water marked paper. Nathan Marks testified that Becker had given him two wrapped packages in August, sealed with wax, to hold for him. Never, he said, had he opened the packages, nor did he know what was in them. This was confirmed by Detective Shaughnessy, who found the stones in Marks's house with the wax seals unbroken.

Because the forged notes had not actually been completed, and had never been passed, Becker was confident from the start that he would not be convicted. Mooney testified that one of the first things

8 NYT, "A Noted Counterfeiter Arrested…"
9 BE, "Becker Sentenced for Life." Aug 30, 1896 http://bit.ly/2i5KQeN

Becker said after being caught was that the police should have "given
him a few weeks more. If you had let me go for a couple of weeks
longer, you might have got something; as it is, there is nothing for
you to take hold of." [10] But he was wrong. When the case went to the
jury on November 30, the presiding judge reminded the jury of the
scope of the term "forgery" for which the defendant was being tried,
which included counterfeiting bank plates with the *intent* to use the
counterfeit in an improper way. It was their charge to determine if
that was the case.

Despite the fact that Becker's lawyer asked the court to charge
sixteen separate propositions to the jury, most of which the court
declined to charge, the jury returned within one hour with a guilty
verdict. On December 14, 1881, he was sentenced to six years and
six months in Kings County Prison. For now, Charlie Becker's run
of luck was over.

---

10   BE, "The Alleged Counterfeiter on Trial for Forgery."

PART TWO

The duties of the middleman being to secure people who would present the forged paper to the banks. For this duty an ex-convict is usually chosen because the testimony of an ex-convict is easier to impeach in case he should turn state's evidence.
—Chicago Daily News *"Big Dan" is an Expert' April 7, 1896*

Confined together, and having continual opportunities of unrestricted conversation, it is natural that the convicts should consummate friendships with, and imbibe the principles of each other. … Convicts who had, mutually, promised to become partners in iniquity, and who had concerted their plans before their liberation, have often been seen waiting for each other, in the very view of the prison, and departing, in company, to practice their villainy.
—*Larry E. Sullivan,* Bandits and Bibles *(p. 103)*

A GOOD AND PLAUSIBLE
TALKER

R ICHARD "DICK" LENOX WAS BORN IN LANCASTER
County, Pennsylvania on January 1, 1833, to Joseph and
Cordelia Lenox. The Lenox family already had a long
tenure in the small town of Mount Joy, having settled there with a
large group of Scots-Irish Presbyterians in the mid to late eighteenth
century. The middle child of three born to Joseph and Cordelia,
Richard had an older brother, Samuel, and a younger sister, Sarah.

In 1850, Richard, already with a young wife and three-year-old
son, was living with his parents in Mount Joy, but in the early 1850s
Joseph began selling his assets in Lancaster County. His holdings
were large for that time period, and one by one he divested himself
of them, as he and Cordelia made plans to pick up and move on.

By 1860, the elder Lenoxes were living in Prairie City, Illinois,
along with their daughter Sarah and her husband, J.C. Gilmer. By
now, Richard had already had his first brush with the law and was
listed in the 1860 census as an inmate at the Hancock County Illinois
jail in Carthage (later made famous by the murder of Mormon leader
Joseph Smith).[1] Hancock County was home to Richard's uncle, James
Lenox, who had moved his family there in the 1840s, and Sheriff
A.T. Helms of Carthage was said to know Dick Lenox well. [2] When
Richard was released he soon made his way back to Pennsylvania,

---

1   1860 U.S. Census, Hancock County, Illinois, population schedule,
Carthage, 420, dwelling 3009, Carthage Jail; digital image, Ancestry.com,
http://ancestry.com
2   WAP to Roger O'Mara, June 10, 1893. Letter. 76-7 PNDA

where he still had family – and no reputation yet. During the next
few years he scrounged a living – legally and illegally – wherever he
could. For a time he worked as a cabbie in Philadelphia [3] and lived
in "disreputable haunts"[4] in the vicinity of Reading Terminal, but
made regular visits back to Lancaster County. On February 16, 1871,
he was brought before a Philadelphia magistrate charged with "con-
spiring to cheat and defraud the firm of Murphy & Sons" of Market
Street.[5] Although he was discharged, he was immediately re-arrested
for attempting to pass a forged draft at the First National Bank on
a New York bank, in the small Lancaster County town of Marietta.
He was put in jail where, as a local newspaper reported "he can pass
many a cold 'draught' down his throat, in the absence of tea, coffee
and other delicacies."[6] The court docket stated that he was single,
could read and write, and had a scar on his head when he was sentenced to "three years separate and solitary confinement at labor" in
the Lancaster County Prison on April 21, for forgery. [7]

Released on December 21, 1873, Lenox drifted around Pennsylvania looking for easy scores, ending up in Venango County where
he was picked up, along with another small-time crook named
George Haley, in early 1876. He and Haley were charged with forgery on Mitchel's Bank in Rouseville, near Oil City and placed in the
Venango County Prison, but managed to escape before they could
be tried.

Lenox and Haley, also known as "One-armed Palmer" or "Captain Palmer," made their way back to Illinois by December, having
worn out their welcome in Pennsylvania. Illinois was always attrac-
tive to Lenox, as he could stay with his family while he planned his

---

3   Ancestry.com. U.S. City Directories, 1822-1995 [database on-line].
Provo, UT, USA: Philadelphia City Directory 1870. www.ancestry.com
4   *Canton Weekly Register*, C.W. Heald, "Lenox the Forger." Aug 5, 1897,
77-6 PNDA
5   *Lancaster Intelligencer Journal*, "Attempted Fraud," Feb 22, 1871.
http://bit.ly/2v1ynKt
6   Columbia Spy, "Marietta Gossip." March 4, 1871
7   Lancaster County (PA) Prison Description Docket, 1851-1887.

next move. His mother, by now a widow, had moved to Hancock County to be near her brother-in-law and his family, but Dick's sister, Sarah Gilmer and her family had settled in Canton, Illinois, just a few counties to the east in Fulton County.

*   *   *

DURING THE FIRST few months of 1877, Lenox and Haley established themselves, and their "good" reputations in and around Hancock, McDonough and Fulton Counties. It is here that we get our first description of Dick Lenox: a tall man at 5 feet 11 ½ inches, with brown hair and eyes, and a mustache. Handsome, with his dark complexion and hair, "a good and plausible talker," Lenox slipped easily into the role of man-about-town. [8] He and Haley spent their time "largely in saloons and resorts for loafers and idlers, recounting remarkable stories of detective experiences, smart schemes for gulling the unsophisticated 'hayseed,' speculative deals in oil fields of Western Pennsylvania and New York...etc. They spent money freely among the frequenters of the places they visited ... often showing drafts for large sums...." [9]

Dick Lenox and his friend Haley were already operating on a model that would become part of the pattern for professional forgers for decades, and that would serve Charlie Becker's gang so well in the future. Thomas Byrnes, in his classic work, *Professional Criminals of America*, laid the plan out clearly:

> Forgers who make a practice of defrauding the banks of the smaller cities, first establish confidence with the officials of the institution they intend to plunder. ... [they make] a number of bona fide deposits and [have] some business transactions, which are simply the transfer of money from one city to another. Then when [they

---

8   History of Richard Lennox alias Heywood.... Manuscript. 78-4 PNDA
9   CWR, "Lenox the Forger."

are] beyond suspicion [they] lay down for collection a draft for a large sum, which bears the forged signature of a genuine depositor at a bank in a distant city. Upon the presentation of the paper the officials telegraph to the bank it is drawn upon, inquiring if the person or firm whose forged signature it bears is a depositor in good standing there. The answer being satisfactory, at least three-fourths of the amount called for by the check is willingly advanced by the bank of deposit.[10]

On April 11, Lenox walked into the Farmers National Bank of Bushnell and obtained $400 on a fraudulent draft, supposedly drawn by Judson's Bank of Ogdensburg, New York on the Fourth National Bank of New York City. He was identified and the draft was endorsed by "a citizen of Bushnell." According to the 1877 edition of Banker's Magazine,

> On the following day [he] got from the First National Bank of Canton, IL – thirty miles east of Bushnell – $600 upon another draft of the same character, being identified through a resident. On the same day, an accomplice known as Captain George Palmer, - a one-armed man – procured at the Home Bank of Canton $500 on a similar draft, he being satisfactorily identified by an old citizen of the place....They had in their possession other drafts of the same description, in various amounts from $400 to $1,500. The drafts were well executed lithograph forms manufactured by Wm. M. Christy's Sons, Philadelphia, very neatly filled out in a business hand, machine numbered, revenue stamp imprinted, and perforated by a "check protector." They were signed in due form, and addressed to the regular correspondent of Judson's Bank....[11]

Immediately after Lenox and Haley cashed the forged checks, they headed east to Peoria, hoping to enjoy their bounty and stay one step ahead of law enforcement. When the banks received word

10   Byrnes, 16

11   1877 *The Banker's Magazine and Statistical Register*, I. Smith Homans 1876-77 v.31, p. 990 http://bit.ly/2wPI40x

the following week that the drafts were all fraudulent, local authorities began questioning everyone who had done business with the
two men, and Lenox's sister and brother-in-law in particular, who
were not inclined to give him up. Sarah destroyed a photograph of
her brother, rather than giving it to the police to aid the chase. [12]
Another photograph was found and sent out to law enforcement
across the country, which eventually bore fruit when the chief of
police in Philadelphia wired in early May that they had apprehended
Lenox on May 11th, and had him in their custody. In the journalistic hyperbole of the day, the Chicago Tribune reported "[t]here is
scarcely a State in the Union in which he is not wanted.... His arrest
will cause great satisfaction to nearly every banking institution in the
whole country." [13]

Lenox, of course, was already well-known in Philadelphia, and
when the chief of police there received the wire from Illinois, he put
the word out to his officers to look for Lenox in his old haunts. They
were quickly successful, as one of the patrolmen in the Reading Terminal area recognized him immediately, having seen him on his beat
that week. Lenox had a reputation for violent resistance and escape,
so when he was next spotted, police took precautions. Several patrolmen in plain clothes surrounded and tackled him. He "charged like
a mad bull and gave them a hard fight," but once they recovered his
gun and a large amount of cash from his pockets, he gave up his resistance and was escorted to the police station and jail. [14]

Police caught a break when Lenox sent for a friend, an unnamed
young man the police already knew and mistrusted. He was immediately arrested as a possible accomplice, and sent for his mother,
with whom he lived, for assistance. The mother was terrified that
her young son would be taken to Illinois along with Lenox, and was
only too happy to tell all she knew of Lenox and Haley, and their

12   CWR, "Lenox the Forger."
13   *Chicago Tribune*, "An Old Offender." May 13, 1877. http://trib.
in/2vILPor
14   CWR, "Lenox the Forger."

movements during the past month. She admitted that the men had
made her house their headquarters that spring, where they formu-
lated their plans to swindle the Illinois banks and made the arrangements that allowed them to do so. Her story was corroborated by the
lithographers who unknowingly prepared the drafts, and the clerk at
the hotel where the woman said the men had stayed. She even was
able to give them a clue as to where Haley had gone – "a town in
Iowa that had two parts to the name." She informed the police that
Lenox and Haley had made their way to Canada the morning after
they arrived back in Philadelphia from Illinois, where they claimed
to have fleeced banks in Montreal and possibly in Toronto, before
deciding to split up and go to ground. [15]

Once word of Lenox's capture was received in Illinois, authorities there quickly arranged to travel to Pennsylvania with the paper
work necessary to bring him back. Lenox had already hired a criminal attorney who was moving for a *habeas corpus* in his case, so time
was of the essence. Peoria's Sheriff Frank Hitchcock and his retinue,
including a bank teller who could identify Lenox, started for Pennsylvania where they stopped in Harrisburg, the capital, to secure
extradition papers from Pennsylvania's lieutenant governor himself
in the middle of the night. [16]

On Monday, May 14, 1877, Lenox and his attorney were ready
for a fight, but the judge quickly passed on the case and, after exam-
ining the extradition papers, turned him over to Sheriff Hitchcock,
who got them on the 12:30 p.m. train to Chicago. Being a wise
lawman, the Sheriff quickly got Lenox some food and medicine, and
generally did everything he could to make Lenox comfortable. He
soon got Lenox talking and before long got a full confession from
him. A full confession that dove-tailed perfectly with the information from the quick-to-talk mother in Philadelphia.

According to Lenox he and Haley, after leaving Illinois, made

---

15   Ibid.
16   Ibid.

a very quick trip to Philadelphia, and then headed north to Canada. In Toronto they followed their usual pattern and employed a scheme identifying themselves as horse buyers, sometimes successfully and sometimes not. From there they headed to Quebec, where they managed to get away with $3000 using similar methods, and then to Plattsburgh, New York, where they were also successful. At that point, they concluded that they were "rich enough to retire from business," and they split up, Lenox heading to Philadelphia "to see his best girl," and Haley to Cedar Rapids, Iowa, where he had a wife. If only he had been let alone, said Lenox, he was going to quit the business of forgery and be honest evermore. In fact, he said, he was just starting out when he was arrested, and his good intentions had therefore been interfered with through no fault of his own! [17]

When Hitchcock discovered that Lenox's arrest had already made the Chicago newspapers, he left Lenox in the custody of a US Marshall who was traveling with them, and quickly made his way to Cedar Rapids to look for Haley before the news of Lenox's arrest reached him. Hitchcock, along with local officials found Haley gardening at his home in "Time Check Valley,"[18] and chased him into the house, where "there was a short, sharp fight; Haley grabbing the crockery from the breakfast table…and throwing anything he could reach viciously at Hitchcock, his wife joining in the battle."[19] After a brief tussle Hitchcock overpowered Haley, and the Sheriff and local lawmen arrested him and escorted him to the Peoria jail, where he was re-united with Lenox. They were soon transferred to the Fulton County Jail, where they awaited trial for their crimes in Canton and Bushnell.

---

17   CWR, "Lenox the Forger."
18   *Cedar Rapids Times*, "More Forgery." May 24, 1877
19   CWR, "Lenox the Forger."

A VERY FUNNY INCIDENT

"BIG DICK" LENOX, AS HE WAS NOW CALLED BY LAW enforcement, and "One-armed Palmer" were sentenced on September 6, 1877, in Fulton County, Illinois for swindling three banks in Canton and Bushnell.[1] Originally sentenced to two and a half years in the Joliet, Illinois penitentiary, Lenox was transferred to the Chester, Illinois, penitentiary on March 21, 1878. He learned to be a "first-class stone-cutter and marble cutter" during his time there, although he also spent a lot of his time in planning and attempting ways to escape.[2]

Lenox was discharged from the Chester Penitentiary on October 21, 1879. Apparently Haley was released around the same time, as they both re-appeared in Philadelphia within a few months, where they took up with other local small-time swindlers. Bank forgeries that bore the *modus operandi* of Lenox and Haley were reported in Montreal, Canada, and several Pennsylvania towns. The group narrowly escaped capture after cheating banks in Emlenton and Edinburg, Pennsylvania in early 1880 before traveling west to try their luck in a new place, outside of Wichita, Kansas.

The two men arrived in Cowley County, Kansas early that spring and established themselves as a man of great wealth (Lenox) looking for a suitable location to establish his crippled brother (Haley) in the stock business. Just as they had done in Canton, Illinois, the men spent money freely and quickly gathered a group of friends and acquaintances around them. They cashed several genuine drafts, of

---

1 Richard Lenox Criminal Record. Document. 78-4 PNDA

2 WAP to Roger O'Mara, June 10, 1893. Letter. 76-7 PNDA

small amount, which gained the confidence of their new friends. Once the drafts were proven to be good and the new friends convinced, they moved in for the kill. After cashing large drafts at Kohn Brothers & Levi, Woodman & Son, and a third bank in Arkansas City, they skipped town sometime in April, 1880.

Lenox made his way back to Philadelphia, where he continued to work with whomever he could convince to help him operate his latest schemes. In October he was behind a plan with a William Phelan, to fleece a bank in York, Pennsylvania. Phelan, a small-town crook who was arrested in October in Philadelphia, admitted to his thievery when brought to trial the next January, but swore "he wouldn't have done it if it hadn't been for Dick." Lenox, he said, "pressed him into it" while they were in town for the York Fair. The two of them had been traveling around central Pennsylvania looking for opportunities, he said, and he had no idea that Lenox was a forger. Phelan was found guilty of the crime, but, of course, Lenox was nowhere to be found.[3]

In the meantime, Kansas authorities had sent out pictures of Lenox and Haley to law enforcement around the country. As fortune would have it, one of the Cowley County "friends" that was duped by Lenox and Haley, a traveling salesman by the name of George Lun, saw Lenox on a March day in Chicago in 1881, and knowing that he was wanted for the crimes in Kansas, notified the Chicago Police. They, in turn arrested Lenox, who was traveling under the name of H.R. LeClair, and notified Cowley County's sheriff, A.T. Shenneman, who made a quick trip to Chicago where Lun was able to identify Lenox. Sheriff Shenneman arrested Lenox on March 27, 1881, and the two of them boarded the next train south.

Seventy-five miles from Kansas City, Lenox proved true to his reputation for recklessness, and audacity, and escaped from custody, jumping off the moving train, in handcuffs, and disappearing. Fortunately for Shenneman, he had removed the contents of Lenox's

---

3   *York Daily*, "Court." Jan 14, 1881

pockets earlier, which included a letter written in a feminine hand from Canton, Illinois and signed, "S." When he arrived back in Kansas, he immediately contacted the police in Canton and learned that Lenox's sister, Sarah, lived in that place and that Lenox was in the habit of visiting her regularly. Soon the Canton postmaster, the marshal of the town and the county sheriff were on the lookout.

Finally, on the night of June 16, 1881, their vigilance paid off. Lenox was seen by the town's night watch driving into Canton. He had been hiding out of town during the daylight, it seemed, and coming in to visit Sarah only after dark. That night, they were ready for him and Lenox was captured. The county sheriff telegraphed Shenneman, who started at once for Illinois. Lenox managed to retain legal counsel immediately, probably through his family connections, and *habeas corpus* proceedings were already in progress when Shenneman arrived the next morning. But the Kansas sheriff was ready, and grabbed the prisoner as soon as he was discharged by the judge. Fighting a local mob that tried to save Lenox, the sheriff managed to slip him into a wagon behind "the fastest team that could be procured," and raced to a train station twenty miles away, where they got on board and finally finished the trip that had begun in March. "This Lennix [sic] proves to be one of the most wily and successful counterfeiters in America," The Winfield (KS) Courier crowed, and "[he] finally got a sheriff after him who never gives up and will keep his eye on him to prevent him from escaping again." [4]

* * *

WITH LENOX SAFELY ensconced in the Cowley County jail, Shenneman set his sights on finding George Haley, who was still on the run. After tracking his route through several states, the sheriff caught up with Haley in Watertown, Wisconsin, in mid-July, where he was operating under the name of Jacob Gross. Shenneman

4 Cowley County Historical Society Museum, Winfield Courier Archives. Digital. http://bit.ly/2whHMCi

arrested Haley and returned with him to Kansas, where he was jailed in Wichita. On August 12th, Haley managed to work the bars of his cell's window out of their sockets and crawl out of the jail. He was quickly found and returned, but the next day, Saturday August 13, was released after a *habeas corpus* ruling. Again, Sheriff Shenneman was ready and re-arrested him, taking him to the Cowley County jail in Winfield on the 15th. There he stayed while the sheriff awaited extradition papers from Pennsylvania, where authorities were waiting to charge him with the 1880 swindles in Emlenton and Edinburg.

On August 20th, Shenneman escorted George Haley 1350 miles back to Pennsylvania, where a $100 reward had been offered for his arrest. Knowing that Haley was charged with swindling both the Emlenton Bank and the Clarion County bank at Edinburg, Shenneman, described as "a quiet, unassuming gentleman," was determined to see justice done in these small Pennsylvania towns as well as his own.

While the sheriff was searching for Haley, Lenox waited for his trial and cooled his heels in the Cowley County Jail. Never an easy prisoner, "Big Dick" at least kept his warders entertained. On July 28 the Winfield Courier reported "a very funny incident" at the jail. Sheriff Shenneman wanted a photograph taken of Lenox, but Lenox was not cooperative. The sheriff went to get the blacksmith, to have Lenox's irons removed so he could have the photo taken, regardless. When they returned to the jail they found Lenox "minus his flowing burnsides and clean shaven. Upon investigation it was found that he had broken the lamp chimney and had shaved himself with the pieces of glass." The picture, needless to say, was taken anyway. In any case, with the figure of a woman and the name "Sallie" tattooed on right arm, and the figures of a man and woman beside a weeping willow on his left, Lenox was pretty easily identified. [5]

*   *   *

5   WAP to Roger O'Mara, June 10, 1893. Letter. 76-7 PNDA

ON NOVEMBER 21, 1881, Lenox was brought to trial where he was convicted of second degree forgery. Not yet fifty years old, Lenox was sentenced to seven years in the Kansas State Penitentiary and so began his third, and to date longest stint in prison. Although he was still a large man, at nearly six feet tall and weighing 175 pounds, his dark hair was beginning to show gray and his collection of scars bore witness to the hard life he had chosen.

A FREE AND EASY
SORT OF FELLOW

O N JUNE 15, 1887, CHARLIE BECKER WAS RELEASED
from the King's County Prison after serving his six year
sentence for the Bank of France forgeries. During his
time there he was a model prisoner, working in the prison shoe shop
and as a "tier man," or the leader of his section of the prison. After
his release, he and Anna rented a house at 78 Bradford Street in
Brooklyn, adjacent to Brooklyn Police Station, where she operated
a boarding house and he supported himself as a painter for a few
months. His father-in-law, Clement Hering, had gotten out of the
active forgery ranks, and Charlie was seemingly "going straight" for
the time being, but under the watchful eyes of the nearby police.[1]
Police Captain Harry French of the Seventeenth Precinct was one of
the Beckers' long-time boarders, and was counted on to keep care-
ful watch on him. In May of 1888, Becker was briefly suspected of
picking up where he left off when some counterfeit Bank of France
notes were found in circulation. The counterfeit notes were so well
done, that the Bank of France was obliged to recall all of its 500
franc notes, and authorities naturally thought Becker was up to his
old tricks. But no evidence was ever found tying Becker to the forgeries. In fact Captain French, interviewed some years later about his
time living with the Beckers, said Charlie "was a good-natured, free
and easy sort of fellow, and one of the best and kindest hearted men
socially that I ever knew." French, who said he did his best to reform

---

1   BE, "Is It Becker?"

Becker during the next seven or eight years, was sure that Becker "was trying to do right."[2]

Sometime that summer of 1887, Charlie Becker opened a saloon at the corner of Atlantic and Pennsylvania Avenues in Brooklyn, which quickly became a watering hole for the counterfeiting and forgery element of the underworld. It was there that Becker began planning what would be the crowning glory of his criminal career, and built a team of con men that would plague law enforcement, challenge the Pinkerton Detective Agency's resources, and move the American Banking Association to make changes to how it did business. Most forgers traced the signature from an authentic document onto the forged paper, but some forgers, like Charles Becker, had enough artistic talent to copy it free hand, so that even the victim couldn't tell it wasn't his own signature. Charlie's talents extended to paper making and expertise in inks and their eradication. Added to his knowledge of lithography and printing, he was a cinch to become one of the best, and most prolific forgers of his time. "Professional" forgery was in its heyday, and Becker was about to become its king.[3]

---

2   *Brooklyn Citizen*, "Becker, The Forger." May 14, 1896 77-5 PNDA
3   Lemert, 98

CANAL BOAT MEN

O NE OF THE MEN OFTEN SPOTTED AT CHARLIE BECKER'S
saloon was a fellow known by the name Bob Bowman.
Born Robert Stockton in 1839, in Ohio, Bowman was the son
of Daniel Stockton and Elizabeth Bowman Stockton. In 1860, the
family lived in Eldorado, Ohio,[1] Robert still living at home along
with a nineteen year old brother, John, and ten year old sister, Elizabeth. But by the end of the decade, things for Bob had begun to go
the wrong direction. He was frequently seen with "canal boat men,"
and by the early 1870s had already developed a reputation as a thief,
safe robber and associate of swindlers and forgers.

Bowman most often associated with boatmen on the Erie Canal
who were also well known to law enforcement, men like Gilbert
"Gib" Yost who had well-developed skills in the forgery line. Born
about the same time as Bowman in Montgomery County, New
York, Yost came from a rather privileged background, was educated
at boarding schools and began law studies before he became a boat-
man on the Canal where he found it much easier to make a living by
passing counterfeit currency and coin.

Sometime in the 1860s Yost became dissatisfied with the small
amounts he was making that way, and began working with a gang
of well-known safe burglars. He was arrested and jailed numerous times for bank and jewelry store robberies in Indiana, New
York and Pennsylvania, including the robbery of a jewelry store in

---

1   1860 U.S. Census, Preble County, Ohio, population schedule,
Monroe, 142, dwelling 1074, Daniel Stockton; digital image, Ancestry.
com, http://ancestry.com

Norristown, Pennsylvania with famed bank robber George Leonidas Leslie in 1870, for which he served two years in prison.[2] After his release, he was part of the famous "Patchen Avenue Gang" of thieves who had set up their headquarters in a mansion on Patchen Avenue in Brooklyn, a gang of expert thieves that included Billy Porter, Johnny Irving, and "Shang" Draper. He was known among criminals and police alike for his personally crafted set of burglars' tools that weighed a mere five pounds, and could be carried in an inside coat pocket without notice.

While Yost was running with the Patchen Avenue Gang, Bob Bowman spent some time in the Auburn (NY) State Prison in the early 1870s, where he met another future confederate named William H. Lyman. Lyman had first been arrested around 1866 in Albany for stealing "a quantity of books in Buffalo," and was sentenced to prison in October of 1868.[3] Born around 1840 as the son of a printer, Lyman was said to be a college graduate and "one of the most skillful men with a pen ever known to the police." He could write the Lord's Prayer in the space of a ten-cent piece, and while he was imprisoned at Auburn, was placed in charge of the prison's books where he was caught "altering the sentence of long term prisoners and letting them out ahead of their time for a consideration."[4]

Lyman was released from Auburn Prison in the early part of 1869, but was arrested again on October 27, 1869 in Albany, charged with the forgery of pardons while imprisoned, and was sent right back to Auburn. This time around, the "consummate rascal" was part of an intricate escape plot, along with several other prisoners, on July 18, 1870. Having hoarded bits of soft solder, supplied by outsiders, they melted it in their prison spoons and used the solder to manufacture a key that could unlock some of the cells. They also fashioned a crude wrench that allowed them to unscrew nuts on the bars of several other cells. Late on that Monday night they put their

---

2   Agency History. Gilbert Yost. 183-9 PNDA
3   *Buffalo Evening Courier and Republic*, Nov 1, 1869
4   NYT, "Ready for Jail Again." Jan 22, 1886. http://nyti.ms/2vIQGpC

escape plan into action by enlarging two stove-pipe holes in a prison chimney, using a quilt to "catch the debris and deaden the sound." The warden, however was onto them, and they were quickly caught and shackled.[5]

Meanwhile Bob Bowman, who had been released from the Auburn Prison, was arrested again in September, 1873, for being in possession of various counterfeit paraphernalia. This time he was sentenced to three years in King's County Penitentiary.

By 1876, Bowman and Lyman were both back on the street. In March, they started off on a forgery spree that kept law enforcement on their tail for the next year and a half throughout New York State and beyond. Always using aliases, of course, the two followed a standard script. They purchased two drafts – one small draft and one large draft, for the amount to which they planned to raise the smaller one. The small one was then altered by Lyman, the expert penman, and the two drafts were made to correspond exactly in amount. Then Bowman would go to a distant community and deposit the altered draft. If there was any suspicion by the depositing bank at all, they could check with the purchasing bank, which would verify a check of that number, in that amount. Once the raised check was successfully cashed, Lyman would return to the purchasing bank with a request to have his money returned on the larger, legitimate draft because he had not been able to use it. It was not until the bank's accounts were reconciled at the end of the month that the trick was discovered [6]

The two started their spree by opening an account with the Yorkville Savings Bank and cashed a number of checks on the National Bank of Newburg, all of which were paid and later found to have been raised. In April they followed the same pattern, opening an account in the Abingdon Square Bank and cashing raised checks from both the National Iron Bank of Falls Village, Connecticut,

---

5   NYT, "Desperate Attempt to Break Jail." July 22, 1870. http://nyti. ms/2v2b6rJ
6   NYT, "More Forgeries Exposed." Oct 5, 1877. http://nyti. ms/2wfd4cN

and the Kinderhook (NY) Bank. Lyman and Bowman then laid low to see what the banks would do. When it was clear that neither defrauded bank was taking any action, they decided it was safe to get back to work. Over the next six months Lyman and Bowman defrauded over a dozen banks and companies, using the same *modus operandi*. According to the second volume of the *Express Gazette* in 1877, these included:

- Leroy National Bank $8.00 raised to $1,450.00; loser American Express Co.
- Marine National Bank Buffalo $12.00 raised to $1,200.00; loser A Johnson & Co.
- Salt Springs National Syracuse small amount raised to $1,900.00; loser US Ex Co.
- First National Bank Bridgeport small amount raised to $1,450.00; a failure
- DA Powers Rochester $10.00 raised to $1,425.00; loser Westcott's Express Co.
- National Iron Bank Morristown $8.50 raised to $1,550.00; not collected
- First National Bank Brockport NY a failure
- Iron National Bank Falls Village Conn $37.79 raised to $1,490.00; loser Third National of NY
- Iron National Bank Falls Village Conn $67.18 raised to $767.78; loser Third National of NY
- Kinderhook National Bank $36.98 raised to $936.00; loser Third National of NY
- Kinderhook National Bank $46.27 raised to $1,646.00; loser Third National of NY
- National Bank of Newburg $38.68 raised to $947.94; loser Abingdon Square and Yorkville Savings Banks
- National Bank of Newburg $14.95 raised to $1,650.27; loser Abingdon Square and Yorkville Savings Banks
- National Bank of Newburg $38.00 raised to $838.00; loser Abingdon Square and Yorkville Savings Banks

- National Bank of Newburg $46.00 raised to $2,700.00; loser Abingdon Square and Yorkville Savings Banks
- National Bank of Newburg $49.17 raised to $3,928.00; loser Abingdon Square and Yorkville Savings Banks
- National Bank of Newburg $28.46 raised to $2,528.00; loser Abingdon Square and Yorkville Savings Banks
- National Bank of Newburg $ 38.29; this check was spoiled by acids
- National Bank of Newburg $ 42.18; this check was spoiled by acids [7]

It was August when the two swindled the American Express Company, and there they met their match. American Express officials immediately contacted the principals of the Pinkerton Detective Agency, who had a pretty good idea of who their suspects were.

On October 3, 1877, both Bowman and Lyman were arrested by Robert Pinkerton – Bowman in a Bowery saloon and Lyman in his Park-Row office, where detectives found all the materials a professional forger might need. The men were confined in the 14th Precinct Police Station until they were transferred to Catskill, New York, where they were indicted for defrauding the American Express Company. Bowman at first plead not guilty, but withdrew his not guilty plea at his February, 1878, trial. Both men plead guilty and were sentenced to four years and six months in Clinton State Prison in Dannemora, New York. [8]

While Bowman and Lyman were cooling their heels in the prison at Dannemora, Gib Yost and his confederates in the Patchen Avenue gang had also been arrested. In August of 1878, the whole crew was caught, and found themselves in Brooklyn's Raymond Street Jail awaiting trial for the burglary of Ibert's Feed Store on Brooklyn's Graham Avenue.[9] Yost originally gave his name as John Doe, later

---

7   The Expressman's Monthly, Volume II January – December 1877 (Cincinnati: James Barclay, 1877) 341 https://goo.gl/Czc8zF
8   R.M. Decker to R.A. McKinney, May 8, 1886. Letter. PNDA
9   NYT, "John Irving Heard From." Nov 6, 1879 http://nyti.ms/2uJ6rzA

changing it to John Wilbur. Yost had a habit of feigning insanity while imprisoned, mumbling and screaming and violently attacking guards. His performance when the Patchen Avenue Gang was arrested in 1878, was so convincing that his jailers pronounced him "mad as a march hare," and by the summer of 1879, he had escaped conviction, sent instead to the State Lunatic Asylum at Auburn. [10]

Both William Lyman and Bob Bowman were released from Clinton State Prison on August 3, 1881.[11] Not ones to stay idle long, they quickly picked up their trade. Out of prison for only six weeks, the two were arrested in Hudson, New York, on September 16th by local authorities and Robert Pinkerton, charged with raising forged drafts on the American Express Company in Fitchburg, Massachusetts, as well as banks in St. Albans, Vermont, and Troy, New York. While they waited in the Catskill jail for a requisition from the Governor of Massachusetts on the American Express forgery, Robert Pinkerton, worked on behalf of American Express to secure the return of the whole amount, which he was able to do. Massachusetts then released the prisoners to the authorities in Troy, where they were tried and convicted in December for their forgery there on bankers Clipperly, Cole & Haslehurst. Back to Clinton State Prison the two went, this time sentenced to four years.

At some point as Lyman and Bowman settled in for their second stay at Clinton, their friend, Gib Yost, who had been released from the Lunatic Asylum, was working on a plan to spring them from the prison. One night he succeeded in passing in to Bowman, who was on the second floor, a set of his famous "miniature" burglar tools to enable Lyman and him to break out. However, the tools were found a day or two later under Bowman's mattress, before they had a chance to implement the rest of their scheme. [12]

*   *   *

10   BE, "Gone Mad." Aug 9, 1879 http://bit.ly/2fM0HPf
11   CT, "His Game Did Not Work." Jan 22, 1886. 77-4 PNDA
12   NYT, "Death of 'Gib' Yost." Aug 12, 1886. http://nyti.ms/2uImldQ

SOMETIME BEFORE THE summer of 1885, Bob Bowman was released from Clinton State Prison. His friend, Lyman, had died in Clinton Prison hospital in November of 1883, of "an inflammation of the bowels after an illness of 10 days."[13] "Gib" Yost, who had been arrested in Chicago for the $15,000 jewelry robbery of E. Veil & Sons in LaPorte, Indiana, was serving time in the Northern Indiana Penitentiary, in Michigan City, Indiana. Even his reputation as "… one of the finest safecracker in the criminal underworld," couldn't save him, and he died there on August 11, 1886.[14] With his two confederates gone, Bowman needed to find some new friends.

---

13   Poughkeepsie Daily Eagle, "Death of Lyman the Forger." Nov 20, 1883 http://bit.ly/2w1Py31
14   J. North Conway, King of Heists (Guilford, CT: Globe Pequot Press, 2009), 178. http://bit.ly/2uJqRJ3

HE DIDN'T GET FAR

During the summer of 1885, the Pinkerton Agency began hearing about forgeries being perpetrated on banks in the Midwest and Southwest United States, and had their suspicions that Bob Bowman, along with some other small-time forgers, was responsible, since the first attempt was in Lima, Ohio, near Bowman's hometown. The crew then went on to swindle banks in Galveston and Houston, Texas, and were suspected in similar escapades in Montana, Oregon, Minnesota and Wisconsin, before hubris tripped them up in Chicago, Illinois.

In December 1885, Bowman, calling himself "George Meeker" bought a consignment of tiles in Elmore, Ohio, and asked that they be shipped to him in Aurora, Illinois. He deposited a draft for $1900, drawn on the First National Bank of Chicago, with the Bank of Elmore and took his receipt. Shortly thereafter he contacted the Elmore bank and requested that the tiles be paid for out of his draft, and that the balance be sent to him in cash. The bank cashier instead sent him a draft for the remainder, and received the following reply:

> If you had sent the currency I would have thought you a good fellow. Since my scheme did not work permit me to sign myself George Meeker [1]

The note naturally aroused the suspicions of the Chicago bankers, and the Pinkerton Agency was called in to investigate.

On January 6, 1886, Bowman, this time calling himself "J.F.

---

[1] WAP to Ed Gaylor, Jan 28, 1892. Letter. 73-7 PNDA

Hale' presented a draft to the Floyd County Savings Bank of Charles City, Iowa, payable to himself and drawn on the First National Bank of Joliet, Illinois. On January 9, he contacted the Floyd County Bank from Chicago and, enclosing his receipt for the draft, asked that the money be sent to him via the United States Express Company, in care of Henry Richards, a local saloon keeper at 119 South Halstead Street. Officials of the Illinois bank knew the draft to be a forgery, and the Pinkerton Agency was ready for "Mr. Hale." The Express Company notified Richards that a package was waiting for him, and that he needed to pick it up in person. When he arrived, he was taken into custody by the detectives, and told them that Hale was waiting back at the saloon where he was quickly apprehended. [2]

One of the Pinkerton agents went to the Commercial House where Bowman had been staying, and discovered a large number of counterfeit checks and certificates drawn on over fifty banks in Bowman's suitcase, some filled out and ready to be used. What their continuing investigation turned up was an ingenious plan on the part of the forgers, one that had worked for at least a few months. It seemed that in the autumn of 1885 three men, including Bowman, had visited a Chicago lithographing business that did a large amount of work for Midwestern banks. Representing themselves as gentlemen who were thinking of opening a bank in the Dakotas, they asked to look at samples of bank stationery, from which they generously helped themselves.[3]

Bowman was taken before a justice on January 21 and bound over for court on charges of forgery and being a fugitive from justice. When his case came up on June 1, he was released on an order of *nolle prosequi* (insufficient evidence) and was discharged. [4] He didn't get far. As he and his attorney made their way out of court, a Pinkerton detective appeared by his side and arrested him on a requisition

---

2   CT, "His Game Did Not Work." Jan 22, 1886 77-4 PNDA

3   Ibid.

4   Professional Criminals of America: Robert Bowman. Typescript. 76-9 PNDA

from the Governor of Vermont on the 1881 forgery on the First National Bank of Brandon, Vermont, the Rutland County National Bank and the First National Bank of Vermont. While Bowman's attorney shouted to him that he had the right to resist, the Pinkerton detective hailed a carriage, threw Bowman in, and raced up LaSalle Street to the Pinkerton Agency, where he was "whisked upstairs."[5] He was then taken to the nearest Illinois Central Railroad crossings and sent back east, where he was committed for trial. He was convicted in Rutland on March 18, 1887, and sentenced, as George Munroe, the alias he used in Vermont, to four more years in prison. [6]

---

5   CT, "Racing Down LaSalle Street." June 2, 1886 http://trib.in/2v28NF0

6   NYT, "A Forger In Trouble." June 4, 1886 http://nyti.ms/2vDGTTs; The State of Vermont, Vermont State Officers Report 1887-88. 1888 http://bit.ly/2fKrv22

ROBERT ALLAN PINKERTON

R. A. & W. A. PINKERTON, PROPRIETORS

PINKERTON'S NATIONAL DETECTIVE AGENCY

Robert A. Pinkerton - 1899

William A. Pinkerton – 1895 (Reproduced with permission -
University of Washington Libraries, Special Collections Division)

Richard Lenox – 1894

Richard Lenox – 1897

Joseph English – 1894

Robert Bowman – ca. 1885

Frank Seaver – 1896

Joseph McCluskey – 1896

Charlie Becker – 1899

James Creegan – 1899

PART THREE

But the chiefest terror of the Pinkerton's [sic] to evil-doers lies in this: they never stop; they never give up a case in which a member of the American Bankers' Association is involved. They will follow even the slightest clues for years, and, almost without exception, they will, sooner or later, run down the criminal and bring him to justice.

—Leslie's Monthly Magazine, *vol. 59 no.6 April 1905 (p.622)*

The only certain way of suppressing professional forgery is to obtain the evidence, arrest and press to conviction and punishment the actual forger. The occasional arrest and conviction of a presenter of forged paper does not stop forgery by "professionals," as a presenter's place is easily filled.

—Annual Report of Pinkerton's National Detective Agency to American Bankers' Association *1895 (p.7)*

NO COMPROMISE

*I*N HIS BOOK, "POLICING THE URBAN UNDERWORLD,"
David Johnson writes that

> "[C]heck and money order forgers were among the most resource-
> ful criminals by the middle of the [19th] century. Fraudulent drafts
> drawn on banks of other cities became so common by the mid-1850s
> that brokers in Philadelphia and New York devised a secret code to
> verify the authenticity of particular notes. The counterfeiting busi-
> ness began to change after 1840 because of technical improvements
> in manufacturing money....The Civil War, by creating an urgent
> demand for a sound national currency, brought the federal govern-
> ment into the battle against this crime. The Treasury Department
> employed the finest engravers available, and their talents provided
> the principal protection against bogus bills until the mid-1860s.
> In spite of the Secret Service's best efforts, counterfeiters with the
> necessary skills and technical knowledge continued to plague the
> nation."[1]

The time between the privatization of the Second Bank of the
United States in 1836, until the National Banking Act of 1863 was
often called the "Free Banking Era," a time when there was no uni-
fied currency, the money supply was very unstable, and state banks
supplied all banking services and regulations. The National Banking
Acts of 1863 and 1864 were intended to create a system of national

---

1   Johnson, *Policing the Urban Underworld*, 52-53

banks, as well as uniform currency, backed by United States Treasury Securities. The Federal Government created the Office of the Comptroller of Currency under the United States Treasury, which was given the authority to examine and regulate all nationally chartered banks. These National Banking Acts were the first step in promoting sounder and more reliable banking practices, but they were unable to avert the Panic of 1873, a worldwide financial crisis that caused banking and businesses failures throughout Europe and the United States.

In January, 1875, two St. Louis bankers came up with the idea of organizing the banks of the United States into "a national fraternity."[2] Interest was so great, that when the first national convention of bankers was held at Saratoga, New York on July 20, 350 bankers representing 32 states and territories were in attendance, and "clearly sensed the importance of concerted effort in the advancement and protection of mutual interests."[3] At their 1876 convention in Philadelphia a permanent organization, The American Bankers Association, was established. During the next eight years, the ABA focused heavily on the issues of resumption of specie payment and bankruptcy laws, but even their president, Lyman J. Gage, admitted that the Association "could as yet point to no distinguished achievement except that of advancing correct ideas."[4]

One of the biggest problems that banks continued to face was fraud, particularly the kind perpetrated by organized gangs of forgers and counterfeiters like Charlie Becker's group. Members of the ABA had been calling for structured protection against fraud since 1881, and the Association's Constitution provided for a Standing Protective Committee of three persons for the purpose of controlling "all action looking to the detection, prosecution and punishment of persons attempting to cause or causing loss, by crime, to any member

2   Wilbert N. Schneider, *The American Bankers Association: Its Past & Present* (Washington, D.C.: Public Affairs Press, 1956), 4.

3   Schneider, 7

4   Schneider, 18

of the Association."[5] But lack of finances kept the Committee from being very effective.

* * *

MEANWHILE, THE PINKERTONS were becoming more and more convinced that unless the Protective arm of the ABA became more robust, the difficulty in preventing criminals like the Becker gang from continuing their escapades would only increase. In a letter to William Pinkerton in March 1894, Thomas G. Conklin, Superintendent of the Kansas City District of the Agency, in referring to Charlie Becker's group, affirmed that "it would look as though the operations of this gang are very extensive and are spreading all across the country: and it would appear that they are getting so extensive that some combined action will have to be taken by the banking institutions in order to protect themselves."[6] And there was precedent.

Private property protection organizations, like private policing, grew out of "the failure of American law enforcement adequately to prosecute certain forms of property crime."[7] In the 1850s, the Merchants' Independent Detective Police was founded to protect its members, and in the mid-1880s, primarily due to the success of criminals like Gib Yost, the wholesale jewelry industry had taken the step of organizing what was known as the Jewelers' Security Alliance, in order to protect their small retailers and punish the burglars who robbed its members. They hired the Pinkerton Detective Agency "to provide specialized detective services," which the Pinkerton Agency already did for the railroads.[8] Based on the success of this Alliance, Robert Pinkerton authored his 1894 article for the North American Review, "Forgery As a Profession." In it, he wrote:

---

5   Schneider, 19
6   T.G. Conklin to WAP, March 26, 1894. Letter. 76-7 PNDA
7   Gilfoyle, 149
8   Ibid.

In my opinion, there is but one way to stamp out professional forgery. Let the banks enter into a union having this for its object. A
union of this kind could be organized and maintained at very little
cost to each member of the Association. When a forgery is perpetrated on a member of this Association, prompt and vigorous action
could then be taken. The first principle of such a union of the banks
should be "no compromise." Arrest the forgers; compel them to dis-
gorge, if possible, but a prosecution to conviction should be certain.
The professional forger would come to understand that in laying
out his plans to commit a forgery, one of the first points for him to
ascertain would be, "Does the bank belong to the American Bankers'
Association for the prosecution of forgers?"

In fact, Pinkerton wrote to the President of the ABA in October,
1894, urging him to use his influence with the officers and dele-
gates "to have favorable action taken" on the matter. "We are convinced," he wrote, "that one or two convictions of leaders of these
forgery gangs, brought about by a Bankers Protective Union, would
do much toward stopping criminals from engaging in professional
forgery."[9]

This was enough for the members of the ABA, and in its report
to the 1895 Convention, the Standing Protective Committee stated
that it had contracted with the Pinkerton National Detective Agency
in December to serve as the Agent of the Association. It was in large
measure the forgeries committed by Becker and his associates that
led them to adopt protective measures, and "inaugurate a crusade
against professional criminals who committed crimes on their members."[10] The report concluded that, as approved by the Protective
Committee, the following was done:

a)   180 photographs and descriptions of professional burglars,
      forgers, sneak thieves and swindlers known to have specially
      been operating against banks were sent to each member.

---

9   RAP to ABA President, Oct 5, 1894. Letter. 76-7 PNDA
10   Report. 77-1 PNDA

These were followed by other photographs and descriptions as we could supply them.

b) To enable criminals to readily determine who were members of the American Bankers' Association, your Protective Committee furnished to each member signs of membership; these signs to be placed over or alongside the tellers' windows and on safes and vaults.

c) An arrangement was made with the publishers of the Bankers' Directory to designate in that publication the banks which were members of your Association.

d) We caused to be circulated among the criminal classes throughout the United States the purpose of the American Bankers' Association to vigorously prosecute without compromise all who committed crimes on its members, and how they could determine who were members of the Association.[11]

With the adoption of these measures, when any one of the Association's members was the victim of an attempted or successful fraud, they were now able to notify the Agency to undertake "the apprehension and prosecution to conviction of the perpetrators of the crime."[12] And it worked. "If there was two banks standin' close together, an' one o' them was a member of the Bankers' Association an' the other one wasn't, the [thieves] 'ud tackle the other one first," said a burglar to turn-of-the-century sociologist Josiah Flynt.[13] Now, the game had changed.

11   Pinkerton's National Detective Agency, Annual Report to American Bankers' Association 1895, 8, in 78-1 PNDA
12   Schneider, 135.
13   Morn, 120

RECONNOITERING

"BIG DICK" LENOX HAD BEEN RELEASED FROM THE Kansas State Penitentiary in 1888, and spent the next several years in and around Philadelphia, probably continuing his work as a sometime cabbie.[1] Bob Bowman had also been released from prison in Vermont. Both men circled in and out of New York City, usually taking rooms in either Manhattan or Brooklyn, where they met with others in their line of work at Becker's and other saloons, as saloons "provided convenient places to discuss plans and to make deals."[2] The police blotters were for the most part silent on Lenox, Bowman and Becker during those years, but letters to and from the Pinkerton brothers noted that a man named Creegan, sometimes going by the name of Howard, was seen with Becker in Jacksonville, Florida, in early 1890, and frequently at Monmouth Park, Gravesend and Sheepshead Bay racetracks. Becker was known by the Pinkertons to be "a perfect slave to gaming," so they knew where to look in order to keep tabs on him.[3] A man of average height and weight, with black hair, brown eyes and a mustache, Creegan was described by New York Police Superintendent George Bangs as "very warm friends and quite chummy," with Becker.[4] Law enforcement also was beginning to have their suspicions

---

1 Sioux City Times, "The Sheriff Brings Him." July 5, 1897 77-6 PNDA
2 Johnson, 11
3 A Partial List of Forgeries by Charles Becker. Report. 78-4 PNDA
4 George Bangs to WAP, April 4, 1894. Letter. 76-7 PNDA

that this man Creegan was now serving as a middleman for Becker's group.[5]

Born in September of 1861, James Creegan was a bit of a dandy. He was always well dressed, and often seen wearing a diamond in his shirt front, or a 4-in-hand necktie. He had been arrested in Baltimore on January 17, 1885 with John Flannigan and John Gilbert (alias Gilbraith) for forging two checks – one on the Howard Bank of Baltimore for $500 and another on the Merchants Bank that was detected as a forgery, and led to their arrest.[6] Indicted and convicted in late January, he was sentenced on February 3 to six years and six months in the Maryland State Prison, under the name of Russe.[7] When Creegan was released in 1888, he made his way to New York City where he was arrested on April 18, 1890, but discharged for lack of evidence. It was then that he joined forces with Charlie Becker, who had just sold his saloon on Atlantic Avenue and was preparing for what would be a five-year tour of crime covering the entire country and swindling dozens of banks out of millions of dollars.

*   *   *

ON JULY 25, 1891, Becker, Bowman and Lenox left New York together, headed to London[8]. Creegan followed on August 6. During the next three months, while the foursome laid plans for their next grand escapade, their comings and goings were being reported back to the Pinkertons. Intelligence sent back included reports on a trip by Lenox and Bowman to Hamburg, Germany to get money changed,

---

5   James McParland to WAP, April 7, 1894. Letter 76-7 PNDA

6   *Professional Criminals of America: James Creegan*. Typescript. 76-9 PNDA

7   Ibid.

8   WAP to J.J.P. Odell, December 27, 1894. Letter. 76-7 PNDA; WAP to John Shore, Jan 15, 1895. Letter. 182-6 PNDA; Report. [Agency History] 78-1 PNDA

and an unsuccessful raid on Creegan by London police. By mid-October, Becker, Creegan and Lenox had disappeared from London, and Bowman wasn't far behind, leaving on October 20. All were back in New York by the middle of November.[9]

Becker's elite forgery crew now consisted of Lenox, Bowman, Creegan, and three other men, Joseph English, Stephen Broadwell, and Dan Benack. They were ready to go on the road by early 1892. The plan was simple. While Becker, as usual, stayed mostly in New York and did the actual forging of paper, teams would spread out across the country, each team consisting of a middleman, who procured genuine checks for small amounts and took them to Becker for alteration, and one or two presenters, who pulled off the actual swindles.

The first banks that were hit were in Cincinnati. Stephen Broadwell, in early February, purchased small drafts from the First National and the Fourth National Banks in Chattanooga, Tennessee. On February 13, he presented a check for $1600 at the German National Bank, and another for $1800 at the Third National Bank of Cincinnati, payable to Thomas Hunt. Both were paid without question. Broadwell, also known as "The Man With the Cough," was a small-time swindler who never quite made it to the big-leagues. With his "steel-grey hair"[10] and short beard, Broadwell played the part of presenter quite well. Often suspected of involvement in various schemes, he had been arrested in November 1880 and imprisoned in the Tombs accused of "having in his possession, with intent to defraud…, counterfeit notes of the Spanish Bank of Havana."[11] He was sentenced in 1881 to five years in Sing Sing Prison, and was well back in the game by the time Becker was regrouping. Broadwell's nickname resulted from the fact that "whenever he presented a draft to be cashed he was invariable [sic] taken with a spasm of

9   [Agency History] 78-1 PNDA

10 NYT, "Clever Detective Work." Nov 19, 1880

11 Ibid.

terrific coughing."[12] And the diversion worked. The cashier at one of the defrauded Cincinnati banks said afterwards that "he paid over the money in a hurry as he feared the man would die at the counter, so violent was the paroxysm of coughing."[13]

After he made it safely away from Cincinnati, Broadwell moved on to Michigan, where in May he secured two small drafts from the Lansing State Savings Bank in Lansing which he presented a few days later, for $1500 and $1800, at the Third National Bank in Detroit. Again he escaped, this time heading back to New York, as the consumption that was the real cause of his cough began to take its toll.

While Broadwell was at work in Michigan, another of Becker's crew was busy defrauding banks in Albany, New York. Dan Benack, who sometimes went by Frank Tefford, was younger than most of his confederates. He was "a New York City boy…Early in his career he was a tugboat captain, but later he became associated with crooks and gained some reputation in New York as a rough burglar…"[14] A large man, he was described in Pinkerton records as "5'9 1/2 or 10"; 200 lbs.; stout build; medium complexion; red hair; good shaped nose somewhat broad at end; coat of arms of the United States Tattooed on left arm and two flags with 'D.B.' tattooed on left arm; bust of woman on shield and two flags on right arm." [15] Probably introduced to the Becker gang by Bob Bowman through his riverboat connections, Dan Benack's tenure in the group was also short. After getting small drafts from the National Spraker Bank in Canajoharie, New York, and the Amsterdam City National Bank in Amsterdam, New York, Benack presented the checks doctored by Becker to the Albany National Bank and the National Commerce Bank, both in

---

12   Police News, "$1,000,000 Stolen By A Gang." Aug 11, 1894 77-5 PNDA

13   Ibid

14   *Chicago Daily News*, "'Big Dan' is an Expert." April 7, 1896. 77-5 PNDA

15   Description. PNDA

Albany, New York, on November 14, 1892, and seemingly got away with it.[16]

While Dan Benack laid low for a while, hoping that his Albany jobs would be forgotten, Steve Broadwell's health declined to the point that he had to stop running. Living with his daughter, he had been confined to bed for four months, which effectively hid him from authorities during the whole time they searched for him. On February 24, 1893, two detectives, "under the pretense of being Inspectors of the Health Department, entered the home at 364 W. 23rd Street in Manhattan, where he was arrested and charged with the forgeries he perpetrated in Cincinnati and Detroit over a year before. The two detectives were assigned to guard him until his health became too precarious.[17] Finally, near the middle of March, he was transferred to the prison ward at Bellevue Hospital, where he died on March 28.[18]

Within weeks, Dan Benack was also captured. On April 1 he was arrested in Knoxville, Tennessee for a bank forgery in that city. Convicted and sentenced on April 5 to three years in the Tracey City coal mines, he escaped, for the time being, paying for his Albany crimes.[19]

Although Benack and Broadwell were out of commission, Dick Lenox and Joseph English made up for their loss to the group.

---

16   Report. 78-1 PNDA

17   NYT, "A Clever Forger Caught." Feb 24, 1893

18   *Decatur Daily Republican,* "Stephen Broadwell, the Noted Counterfeiter…" Mar 29, 1893 and New York, New York City Municipal Deaths, 1795-1949," database, FamilySearch (http://bit.ly/2fEJ8QO: 20 March 2015), Stephen C. Broadwell, 28 Mar 1893; citing Death, Manhattan, New York, New York, United States, New York Municipal Archives, New York; FHL microfilm 1,412,519

19   Although Benack was released in the spring of 1896 for his Tennessee crimes, the Albany police, along with the Pinkertons, were waiting for him. He was re-arrested on April 6 for his fraud in New York State, and imprisoned in the Albany Correctional Facility, where he died in the Penitentiary hospital on December 15. Robert Pinkerton commented that he was sorry to hear of his death. "He was," he said, "simply a tool in the hands of Becker" (RAP to Thomas Willard, December 19, 1896. Letter. 76-8 PNDA).

Between 1893 and 1895 they, along with Bob Bowman, defrauded dozens of banks across the country, and managed to keep one step ahead of Pinkerton detectives for nearly two years.

BUSY IN THE HEARTLAND

W HILE PINKERTON DETECTIVES AND LOCAL LAW enforcement were chasing down the low-hanging fruit like Dan Benack and Stephen Broadwell in early 1893, Bob Bowman, Joseph English and Dick Lenox were busy in the heartland.

Joseph English was born on March 25, 1830, in New York State, the son of Joseph and Elisabeth English.[1] In 1850, the family was living in Onandaga County, and nineteen year old Joseph was listed in the census as a shoemaker.[2] But by the 1860 census, young Joseph had already begun his life of crime, and was enumerated as an inmate at the Auburn (NY) State Prison, imprisoned for the crime of forgery.[3] He had been indicted for forgery in the 2nd degree, and pleaded guilty to forgery in the 4th degree. Charged specifically with passing a counterfeit $5 bill on the Wooster Bank of Danbury, Connecticut, he was sentenced to 2 years in State Prison.[4]

On September 17, 1873, English was arrested again, on the canal boat *Joe Travis* between Piers 44 and 45 on the East River with two other men, "having in their possession molds for manufacturing counterfeit 3 and 5 cent nickel coins, along with about $10 worth

---

1 Tom Davis to H.S. Mosher, May 8, 1941. Letter. 76-11 PNDA

2 1850 U.S. Census, Onandaga County, New York, population schedule, Camillus, 226b, dwelling 27; digital image, Ancestry.com, http://ancestry.com

3 1860 U.S. Census, Cayuga County, New York, population schedule, Auburn Ward 4,246; digital image, Ancestry.com, http://ancestry.com

4 NYT, "Burglars, Forgers and Other Criminals Disposed Of." Jan 14, 1860 http://nyti.ms/2waF0za

in unfinished nickels."[5] One of his cohorts turned state's evidence, and English was sentenced in November to three years in the Kings County Penitentiary.[6]

He couldn't have been out long when he was arrested again in September 1877 by the New York City Municipal Police force for having in his possession and attempting to sell a stolen $1000 "5-20" bond (a government issued bond that matured in twenty years, but was redeemable in five years) for $250.[7] He was convicted on December 14, 1877, and sentenced to seven years at hard labor back in Kings County Penitentiary. As he headed back to Kings County for a second time, he was described as "5'6";140 lbs.; dark brown hair; blue eyes; reddish-brown mustache; sallow complexion; size 7 feet; very round shouldered, 'so much so it appears like a hump'; sharp cheek bones; low forehead."[8] At 47 years old, he was starting to look like a man who had already seen his share of hard times. It was during his second stint at Kings County, that he met Charlie Becker, who began his sentence in 1881 for the Bank of France forgeries. When Becker was released from prison in 1887 and opened his Brooklyn saloon, English, who had been out of prison for four or five years, was ready to come on board.

In January, 1893, English, Bowman and Lenox purchased small drafts of $18 each at three banks in Beatrice, Nebraska. The county seat of Gage County, it was a small town, but was growing rapidly since the Chicago, Rock Island and Pacific Railroad came through in the late 1880s. [9] Rapid growth meant lots of new faces, so the presenters probably thought it was a safe place to run their scam. The Nebraska National Bank, First National Bank, and German

---

5   NYT, "Counterfeiters Arrested." Sep 18, 1873 http://nyti.ms/2i5LtFb
6   NYT, "An Old Counterfeiter In Custody." Sept 5, 1877 http://nyti.ms/2fLaFAa
7   RAP to WAP, May 11, 1893. Letter. 76-7 PNDA
8   Ibid.
9   Alley Poyner Macchietto Architecture P.C., Reconnaissance Level Survey for Beatrice Nebraska Historic Building Survey 2010 (Omaha, Nebraska, 2010), 7

National Bank provided the small drafts to representatives of the group without a thought. Sometime in April Lenox showed up in Omaha, where he presented the drafts, raised to $1,800 each, to three banks in the much larger city, making off with a neat total of $5,400. Not a bad return for a little bit of patience and a few days' work. The Pinkertons were certain that Lenox, English and Bob Bowman, as the presenters, were working with Becker, but as yet didn't have what they needed to arrest them and make it stick. Somehow, the original small drafts purchased by the men were being relayed to Becker for expert forgery before being cashed

The men headed east as quickly as possible, where they split up, Lenox heading for St. Louis, and English making for Topeka, Kansas. "Big Dick" probably obtained small drafts from banks that he came across along the way, and in St. Louis he cashed them at three different banks, Fourth National Bank, Laclede National Bank and US National Bank, for $1,800, $1,600 and $1,500. Meanwhile, English got his small drafts from the Bank of Topeka, First National Bank, and Mr. Guildford Dudley, a private banker in Topeka. Then he headed to Kansas City, Missouri, where three raised drafts were passed at the Midland National Bank, Metropolitan National Bank and Citizens National Bank, each for $1,500.[10] Having cleared nearly $15,000 in four months, with no indication of immanent capture, the men decided to take a break and head back to the east coast. On July 5, 1893, Pinkerton Superintendent R.J. Linden reported that Lenox was spotted in Philadelphia, and that he was known to have met several times with a man named "Bowman" from New York. Linden's sources also reported that Lenox had left for the Adirondacks on July 2.[11] In late August, he was seen in New York by Pinkerton operatives, coming out of a building on Wall Street.[12] By now aged 60, and with a substantial "career" history, Lenox was easily identified by law enforcement. At nearly six feet, a relatively

10   Report. 76-7 PNDA
11   R.J. Linden to RAP, July 5, 1893. Letter. 76-7 PNDA
12   Report. 78-3 PNDA

tall height for a man in that day, his "long nose, long legs, ink tomb and man [on his] left arm [and] female named Sallie on his right," he stuck out in a crowd, which is probably why he knew he needed to keep moving.[13]

As Lenox and English were heading back East, Bob Bowman went west and was soon busy in California. After obtaining three small drafts from Farmers Bank in Fresno ($38), the Bank of Butte County in Chico ($55), and private banker Herbert Kraft in Red Bluff ($65), Bowman moved up the coast to San Francisco where on May 10 he cashed three altered drafts at the London, Paris & American Bank, the Bank of California, and the London & San Francisco Bank. Again, the forgeries were so expertly done that even banker Kraft, when shown the altered draft under a magnifying glass said it was not possible that it had been raised, and thought perhaps he might have made a mistake "and written the paper for $6500 instead of $65."[14]

The men seemed to be hidden from view for the remainder of 1893, so the detectives bided their time and continued their talks with the American Banking Association, knowing that it wouldn't be too long before the lure of easy money would draw the four out again. They didn't have long to wait. Lenox, Bowman and English went back on the road as soon as 1894 arrived. They had big plans, but by this time, law enforcement and the American Banking Association were ready for them.

With the actions taken by the ABA, the Pinkerton brothers were convinced that they were well on the way to taking down the Becker gang. In October, 1894, Robert wrote to William (and copied to all other Pinkerton offices) enclosing a copy of a letter that went to the presidents of all the Association's banks including a "partial" list all the forgeries, as far as they were known, of the Becker gang since 1892. Partial, because he knew, as did the thieves, that bankers didn't

13   WAP to Roger O'Mara, June 10, 1893. Letter. 76-7 PNDA
14   William B. Meloney. [n.t.][1902?] 77-9 PNDA

always report thefts of this kind, preferring not to let the public know they had been duped. He included separate lists of the banks from which drafts had been purchased, as well as banks where the altered drafts had been presented.[1] The letter made it clear to the bank presidents that "the manner in which the forgeries were committed… together with other circumstances make it more than reasonably certain that Becker done [sic] the actual forgery work on all the forged paper presented at these banks…. There are many other forgeries with which Becker was connected that have never been made public and some of which although known are not made public for the reason the banks operated on have suppressed it and requested that the same be suppressed."[2] This "partial" list[3] was still extensive:

DATE	BANK	AMOUNT	RESULT
Apr. 10, 1877	Union Trust Co., NYC	$64,000	Successful
Feb. 10, 1892	Third Nat'l Bank, Cincinnati, O.	$1,800	"
Feb. 10, 1892	German Nat'l Bank, Cincinnati, O.	$1,600	"
Aug. 26, 1892	Merchants Nat'l Bank, Cincinnati, O.	$1,500	"
Apr. 12, 1892	Nat'l Commercial Bank, Albany, NY	$1,600	"
Apr. 12, 1892	Albany Nat'l Bank, Albany, NY	$1,500	"
Oct. 17, 1892	Industrial Trust Co., Providence, RI	$1,400	"
Oct. 1892	First Nat'l Bank, Richmond, VA	$2,100	"
Apr. 28, 1893	Metropolitan Nat. Bank, Kansas City, MO	$1,500	"
Apr. 28, 1893	Midland Nat. Bank, Kansas City, MO	$1,500	"

1   RAP to WAP, Oct 10, 1894. Letter. 76-7 PNDA
2   Ibid.
3   Ibid.

DATE	BANK	AMOUNT	RESULT
Apr. 28, 1893	Citizens Nat'l Bank, Kansas City, MO	$1,500	"
Apr. 29, 1893	Fourth Nat' Bank, St. Louis, MO	$1,800	"
Apr. 29, 1893	Laclede Nat' Bank, St. Louis, MO	$1,600	"
Apr. 29, 1893	U.S. Nat'l Bank, St. Louis, MO	$1,500	"
Apr. 30, 1893	Omaha Nat'l Bank, Omaha, NE	$1,800	"
Apr. 30, 1893	First Nat'l Bank, Omaha, NE	$1,800	"
Apr. 30, 1893	Nebraska Nat'l Bank, Omaha, NE	$1,800	"
May 10, 1893	Bank of California, SF	$8,500	Confidential
May 10, 1893	London, Paris & American Bank, SF, CA	$3,800	"
May 10, 1893	London, Paris & American Bank, SF, CA	$5,500	"
Aug., 1893	Security Nat'l Bank, Minneapolis	$2,200	Deny It
Aug., 1893	Continental Nat'l Bank, Chicago, IL	$3,000	Successful
Sept. 1893	First Nat'l Bank, Chicago, IL	$1,400	Failure
Jan. 18, 1894	Union Nat'l Bank, New Orleans, LA	$1,800	Successful
Jan. 18, 1894	Peoples Bank, New Orleans, LA	$2,100	Successful
Jan. 18, 1894	New Orleans Canal & Banking Co., New Orleans, LA	$1,900	"
Jan. 31, 1894	Merchants Nat. Bank, Providence, RI	$1,800	"
Feb. 1, 1894	Second Nat'l Bank, Providence, RI	$1,800	"
Apr. 1894	Valley Nat. Bank, Des Moines, IA	$1,600	"
Apr. 21, 1894	Corn Exchange Nat. Bank, Sioux City, IA	$1,800	"

DATE	BANK	AMOUNT	RESULT
Apr. 1894	Iowa State Bank, Sioux City, IA	$2,200	"
Apr. 1894	Security Nat'l Bank, Sioux City, IA	$1,800	"
March 9, 1894	Fort Worth Nat'l Bank, Fort Worth, TX	$1,600	"
April, 1894	Nat'l Bank State of Florida, Jacksonville, FL	$1,600	"
April, 1894	Nat'l Bank State of Florida, Jacksonville, FL	$1,500	"
April 26, 1894	Milwaukee Nat. Bank, Milwaukee, WI	$1,800	"
April 26, 1894	Nat'l Exchange Bank, Milwaukee, WI	$1,800	"
May 12, 1894	Third Nat'l Bank, Detroit, MI	$1800	"

Even though they had arrested quite a few of the presenters that Becker was using, the detectives could see that there was no slowdown in the gang's work. The brothers were intent on stopping Charlie and the others, and were sure that by getting the cooperation of all the banks in the Protective Association to be vigilant, they would finally be successful.

A DESPERATE MAN

IN JANUARY, 1894, BOWMAN AND LENOX HEADED TO THE Deep South where Bowman purchased small drafts at two banks, one in Natchez, Mississippi and the other in Vicksburg. On January 18th the two raised drafts were passed by Lenox in New Orleans, Louisiana, one at the New Orleans Canal and Banking Company, the other at Union National Bank. By February, Bowman was back on the east coast, where he purchased a small draft at the National Eagle Bank in Bristol, Rhode Island, which was raised and passed at the Second National Bank in Providence shortly afterwards. Lenox was spotted in Florida in late March when his attempt to cash a fraudulent draft on the First National Bank of Florida as R.L. Goodwin, one of his common aliases, was thwarted.[1]

Spring was busy for the two men. In April, Lenox purchased drafts in Huron, South Dakota from the National Bank of Dakota, and from a bank in Mitchell, South Dakota. Both were raised and passed by "Big Dick" in Sioux City, Iowa, one at the Corn Exchange National Bank, the other at the Security National Bank. He and Bowman worked in tandem on the next job. Bowman purchased two drafts in Stevens Point, Wisconsin and Lenox proceeded east to cash them in Milwaukee.

During this period small drafts were also purchased at banks in Avoca, Iowa and Audubon, Iowa, attributed to the gang, but they were never cashed. [2] Then in early April a draft in the amount of $16 was purchased at the Atlantic National Bank in Atlantic, Iowa.

---

1   Take Warning!! March 27, 1894. Postcard. 76-7 PNDA
2   Job Card to WAP, May 5, 1894. Letter. 76-7 PNDA

On April 20th it was cashed for $1600 at Valley National Bank in Des Moines. Most of the banks in the Midwest, by this time, were on the lookout for members of the group, alerted by notices from the Pinkertons, as well as bulletins from the ABA. Lenox's height, at 5 feet 11 inches, was often a tipoff to his identity. English was even easier to spot with his stooped posture – "almost the appearance of a hunchback" – peculiarly shaped head and lack of two fingers on one of his hands.[3]

When the large draft was cashed at the Des Moines bank, the cashier notified the bank president, J.J. Town, who alerted authorities, and the man who cashed the check was immediately arrested. Described by Town in a letter to William Pinkerton as "possibly 5 ft. 7…, forehead not high and slightly receding…somewhat round shouldered, third finger of right hand gone and little finger appeared to be crooked and stiff [and] position standing is slightly stooping," Pinkerton knew they had captured Joseph English.[4] English, with James Creegan, had been spotted by Pinkerton operatives on April 12 in New York City, coming from "the direction of the Ferry," undoubtedly back east to bring the small drafts to Becker for alteration.[5] When a photograph of the presenter was sent back to Robert Pinkerton in New York, he confirmed that one of his operatives was able to positively identify him as English.[6] Joseph English was indicted before a grand jury, and pleaded guilty to a charge of uttering forged paper, but "refused to divulge any connection he might have in the business…"[7] His attorney argued for a light sentence due to English's age, but the judge didn't see "a single extenuating circumstance."[8] He was sentenced on June 4 to twelve years in prison. He entered the Iowa State Penitentiary at Ft. Madison, Iowa on June

---

3   Report. [77-1] PNDA

4   J.J. Town to WAP, May 2, 1894. Letter. 76-7 PNDA

5   W.H. Minster, April 12, 1894. Report. 78-3 PNDA

6   RAP to WAP, May 3, 1894. Letter. 76-7 PNDA

7   WAP to RAP, June 9, 1894. Letter. 76-7 PNDA

8   Ibid.

8. At 64 years old, some thought he would spend the rest of his life behind bars.[9]

While English was busy in Iowa, Dick Lenox was in Milwaukee, preparing to cash the drafts that Bowman had gotten in Stevens Point. On June 24th, 1894, he took one to the National Exchange Bank, and the other to the Wisconsin National Bank. The banks in Wisconsin were prepared, though, as had been the ones in Iowa. The Pinkertons had anticipated an attempt by the group in larger cities like Milwaukee, and had provided descriptions and photographs of the swindlers, including Lenox, to local banks. But before the authorities could capture him, the ever-slippery Lenox managed to get out of town. This time, he headed for Absecon, New Jersey, near Atlantic City, and holed himself up on a small farm, where he managed a few weeks of liberty, until the law caught up with him. He may have been safe there for some time, if a local confederate had not accidently mentioned him, and his location, to a member of law enforcement. A group of local New Jersey officers, along with several Philadelphia detectives who knew Lenox, set out for the farm on July 6th. As a local newspaper reported it, "Knowing him to be a desperate man and a hard fighter, a posse was organized…to secure him. They went to his farm one night, but were not successful in surprising him. A hot battle followed, during which a fusillade of shots took place…. Lenox was finally caught, [and] the handcuffs put on him…[10] They took him to the jail in Atlantic City, where they waited for him to be requisitioned by Wisconsin.[11] On July 8, he was extradited to Wisconsin where he spent nearly a year in a Milwaukee jail awaiting trial and doing his best to avoid prosecution.

While he was cooling his heels in the Milwaukee jail, Lenox had a visit from William Pinkerton. Having captured both Lenox and English, the detectives were confident that they were well on

---

9   Tom Davis to H.S. Mosher, May 8, 1941. Letter. 76-11 PNDA

10   NYT, "Forger Lennox Again a Prisoner." July 1, 1897. 77-6 PNDA

11   *Atlantic City Review*, "Old Dick Lennox Caught Napping." July 3, 1897 77-6 PNDA

their way to breaking up the gang and, ultimately, capturing Charlie Becker, the brains and forger extraordinaire, and it was time to get down to business. On Saturday, December 22, Pinkerton traveled by train from his office in Chicago to Milwaukee, where he had previously arranged with the Chief of Police to have an extended private interview with Lenox. He hoped to get something from Lenox that would implicate Becker and the others, although Chief Janssen had little hope of that. Lenox was quite morose by now according to the Chief, stubborn and "very hard to get anything from at all."[12] Lenox's attorney, a man by the name of A. C. Brazee, had spent the months since Lenox's arrest trying to track down Bowman or Becker in the hope that they would "stand up" for him, but neither had been found. By now, Lenox was "very sore at Becker and the balance of the gang abandoning him in Milwaukee..."[13] Pinkerton, knowing the ways of crooked men, saw this as an opportunity to get Lenox talking, and was eager to meet with him.

When Janssen brought a reluctant Lenox in, Pinkerton said "Well I have come here to have a plain, everyday talk with you. I am not seeking in any way to entrap you or to make you any further trouble. You have trouble enough, God knows, without any more coming from me. All I want to do is to try and get from you something to land Chas. Becker and Bowman, the men who have deserted and left you in as bad a boat as you are. If through your efforts I succeed in getting anything of the kind, then possibly through my efforts I may be able to aid you in the way of mitigation of punishment. If, however, you don't see fit to give me any information, you must bear in mind that there are at least six other places where they identify you, and you cannot expect to get out of this trouble very easily.....The Becker-Bowman crowd have not done anything for you. It has always been their rule when a man got into trouble to [leave] him to paddle his own boat. They have done this in every case

---

12   WAP to J.J.P. Odell, Dec 27, 1894. Letter. 76-7 PNDA
13   WAP to John Shore, January 15, 1895. Letter 182-6 PNDA

you can name."[14] Pinkerton went on to tell Lenox about the banking association that was at that moment being formed by "the leading bankers of the Country… to put a quietus on professional forgery" altogether.[15] Perhaps even more convincing to Lenox, he told him that Joe English's wife was "starving to death" in the east, and had never received a single dollar of assistance from the others. Lenox had heard that as well, and claimed to himself have sent English's wife money through Bowman, whom he cursed roundly.

Then Pinkerton dropped his most effective piece of information. Bob Bowman, he told Lenox, "had been a 'stool pigeon' for detectives all his life" and he could prove it by producing handwritten letters from Bowman, letters that affected Lenox, Becker and all the others. He told Lenox that Bowman had accompanied the group at the Pinkertons' behest on their trip to Europe in 1891 in order to have them "thrown down." Pinkerton asked Lenox if he was willing, now, to have a talk with him. Lenox wanted to see his lawyer first, and after about ten minutes with Brazee, came back into the room. Pinkerton plied him with a bit of whiskey, and he agreed to talk.[16]

> Dick said: "You remember the forgeries which took place at New Orleans about a year ago on the Becker system?" I said, "Yes, I recollect this very well." "Well," he said, "you know old Bowman won't go to the front and put down a piece of paper. You can't drag him up to do it.…Well Bowman got the small drafts from banks in Vicksburgh[sic], Natchez and Jackson, Miss., that were used in the forgeries at New Orleans, and he can be identified for that." He wound up eventually by saying that Bowman also got the small drafts on which the forgeries were committed in the case which he (Lenox) was now arrested for, at Stevens Point, Wisconsin, and he said: "You can put it down for a fact that every piece of paper that I have ever passed I got from Bowman, and he got the small drafts from which the large drafts were made."

---

14   WAP to J.J.P. Odell, Dec 27, 1894.
15   Ibid.
16   Ibid.

Lenox told Pinkerton that in their trip to Europe in 1891, he knew they got $20,000 at Leeds, England, that he read the account of a forgery committed in that city and that he knew Becker was the head of it because it was talked over when he was in Europe with them two or three years ago.[17] Lenox went on to tell Pinkerton that Bowman was living in Roselle, New Jersey, and going by the name of Gilman. He talked about Creegan, saying he was "the closest friend Becker has got, and to get Becker you have got to get to [Creegan]. [Creegan] is his 'shadow' and is with him constantly. That he don't [sic] think [Creegan] 'puts down' any checks, but he assists in preparing paper and doing things of that sort. He said: '[Creegan] is an exceedingly smart, fly man and would be very hard to work."[18] The only place Lenox knew of him frequenting was a saloon at the corner of Fulton and Broadway in New York. Of course, Lenox said he never got any forged paper directly from Becker and "could not harm him if he wanted to."[19] When Pinkerton asked him where Becker and Creegan were, Lenox said the men were race horse friends and likely to be anywhere the horses were running. He thought the men both lived in the Brooklyn neighborhood of Williamsburg, and that they frequently spoke about a policeman in the vicinity who kept them posted of anyone who appeared to be watching their houses. Lenox was eager to offer to take the witness stand against Bowman and, after a few more shots of whisky, shared more tall tales of his escapades. The interview ended with Pinkerton telling Lenox he may want to talk with him again. "Well, I will talk and talk freely," said Lenox, but the surly tone he used, thought Pinkerton, suggested that he would only talk because he had to.[20]

By the summer of 1895, Lenox still had not been tried for the Milwaukee forgeries. In August, his attorney was seen in New York, as reported by a Pinkerton informant, where he was still trying to

17   Ibid.
18   Ibid.
19   Ibid.
20   Ibid.

find Bob Bowman or Charlie Becker, presumably to get help for
Lenox. The informant told D.C. Thornhill, a Pinkertons Assistant
Superintendent, that he heard that Brazee wanted the word put out
that unless Becker and Bowman came forward and did something for
Lenox soon, Lenox would squeal and implicate them both.[21] Finally,
on September 17, 1895, Lenox was tried and convicted of the Wisconsin forgeries, and given the "very light sentence"[22] of two years
in the Milwaukee House of Corrections. His sentence was not without controversy, and rumors flew that Lenox had "friends in high
places," specifically his attorney A. C. Brazee who had recently been
appointed District Attorney, and who was trying to obtain a pardon
for him. On September 26th, William Pinkerton wrote Superintendent Bangs in New York City that he had filed "a very strong protest"
with the Governor of Wisconsin, lest any effort in that direction
were made.[23] Governor W.H. Upton replied to Pinkerton the next
day, saying that he would bear in mind Pinkerton's request regarding
Lenox that "a little further seclusion – while it might not tend to his
ameniment [sic] morally – would be a preventive to his commission
of further acts of criminality."[24] Even the current President of the
ABA, J. P. Odell, got into the act. In a lengthy letter to Governor
Upton, Odell protested a man with Lenox's history being "let off"
with the light sentence of two years in the House of Corrections
instead of the State Penitentiary. "The American Bankers' Association," wrote Odell, "…through Pinkerton's National Detective
Agency, has gone to a great deal of trouble and expense in looking
up the history and record of this man. I have been advised an effort
will be made to obtain a pardon for him… and I write this letter to
protest against such pardon…. We are particularly anxious about
this matter owing to the fact that members of our Association have

---

21   D.C. Thornhill, Aug 8, 1895. Report. 78-3 PNDA
22   Pinkerton's National Detective Agency, *First Annual Report to
American Bankers Association*, Oct 9, 1895. Abstract. 77-5 PNDA
23   WAP to George D. Bangs, Sept 26, 1895. Letter. 76-8 PNDA
24   Wm. H. Upham to WAP, Sept. 27, 1895. Letter. 76-8 PNDA

requisitions to take this man to other cities where he has committed forgeries, as soon as his time in Milwaukee expires."[25] In the end, no pardon was granted, and Dick Lenox settled into two years at the House of Corrections, knowing that the Pinkertons, and the ABA, would be waiting for him when he got out.

25   J.J.P. Odell to Wm. H. Upham, Oct 5, 1895. Letter. 76-8 PNDA

WORKING AGAINST
OLD FRIENDS

B Y THE TIME WILLIAM PINKERTON REVEALED TO Lenox that Bob Bowman had been stooling for the Pinkertons for years, Becker was probably suspicious of him. Bowman had been captured by Des Moines police in June, 1894, for the New Orleans jobs, where he bought a draft in Vicksburg on Mutual National Bank of New Orleans for $18 and raised it to $1800. When he was never tried for the crime, and disappeared from sight, Becker would have known that the con man Bowman had actually been conning him, Becker, the whole time.

"The informer system," says Frank Morn in *The Eye that Never Sleeps*, "was based upon the personal contacts and friendships cultivated by the detective…the public generally accepted such a system as necessary in crime fighting, because the links between police and criminal seemed so casual."[1] Bowman's relationship with the Pinkertons, and law enforcement in general, was a complex one, as all stool pigeon relationships naturally are. Always weighing his loyalties and his prospects, Bowman sometimes benefitted his comrades, sometimes law enforcement. His primary interest was in benefitting himself, so his boundaries were permeable. The Pinkertons were probably using him as early as the 1880s, and he was already reporting on Becker's movements by spring of 1891.[2] He worked for the Pinkertons on a case involving the Drexel Morgan banking house and, as William Pinkerton told Lenox, was planted with the Becker gang

---

1   Morn, 141
2   Bob Bowman to Pinkertons, April 15, 1891. Letter. 76-7 PNDA

in the summer of 1891 when they traveled to Europe.³ In an 1893 letter to the Chief of Police in Omaha, Nebraska, Robert Pinkerton asked that a picture of Bowman not be shown around too much, and when it was shown, not to reveal his identity as "it might injure some matters we are working on in this city [New York] in connection with this gang... [W]e are investigating some circumstances in connection with this gang and we are not in a position at the present time to have any exposure made."⁴

The Pinkertons also tried to use Bowman to implicate and capture a notorious thief, "Fritzie" Dhien around the same time. Dhien was suspected in the robbery of nearly $20,000 worth of diamonds from a jewelry salesman on the train from Dayton, Ohio to Cincinnati on November 10, 1891. Since he was from the Dayton area, Bowman was the perfect plant in the Dhien case, or so the Pinkertons thought. Dhien was arrested on December 13, 1891 and scheduled for trial, but he jumped bail and wasn't recaptured and tried until 1894.⁵ The Pinkertons always believed that Bowman had tipped Dhien off, and in fact, Bowman admitted as much in a letter to Dayton Police Chief T.J. Farrell, which Farrell forwarded on to the Pinkertons. Bowman desperately wanted to get back in the good graces of his hometown law enforcement so he could visit his family without being "ashamed to be seen." He did, he said, "assist Dhien to leave Dayton. I did it because I was vexed with Pinkertons for not giving me steady employment. They are just using me as a tool to work against old friends."⁶ The Pinkertons' trust in him was beginning to erode. The Agency kept him under surveillance and operatives filed multiple reports in the summer of 1894 of his activities, mostly visits to various saloons, in the New York City area where he

3   RAP to WAP, July 3, 1899. Letter. 76-9 PNDA
4   RAP to W.S. Seavey, Dec 4, 1893. Letter. 76-7 PNDA
5   WAP to Edward Gaylor, Jan 28, 1892. Letter. 73-7 PNDA
6   Bob Bowman to T.J. Farrell, Nov 1894. Letter. 76-7 PNDA

was, as Dick Lenox had reported, living in Roselle, New Jersey as Mr. Gillman.[7]

In addition to his lack of trustworthiness, Bowman's physiognomy now made him so identifiable that he was beginning to be of less use to the gang and even, perhaps, to the Pinkertons, than he had up to now. Just over 50 years old by now, Bowman was described in Pinkertons' criminal files as:

> [A]bout 5 feet 9 or 10 inches in height, slim build, stoop shouldered, has very large hump on back, weight 150 pounds, complexion fair, at times has good color, dark gray hair, usually trimmed pretty short, mustache dark, whiskers dark gray, worn Dundreary style,[8] chin clean shaven, features sharp, rather long and narrow, face thin- has a very noticeable stoop almost making him look humpbacked and unless he straightens up he might look to be 5 feet 7 inches in height. The stoop or hump is on the left side, he usually carries his head on one side, bald on front of head, scars on bridge of nose and between shoulder blades.[9]

Despite their concerns, the Pinkertons used Bowman again in the summer of 1895 when the remaining Becker gang members made another trip to England, probably knowing that Lenox, and perhaps English, were squealing. They stayed for several months before Becker returned to the United States. But this time, Bowman remained behind, knowing that his currency with both his pals and the Pinkertons was running low.

With his middleman Bowman gone, and his two best presenters captured and jailed, Becker turned to his "shadow," James Creegan, who now became the middleman for the gang, and took the responsibility for finding a few more plausible presenters.

---

7 Report. July 1894. 78-3 PNDA

8 Dundreary style were long, full sideburns after the sideburns worn by actor Edward A. Sothern as Lord Dundreary, a character in the play *Our American Cousin* (1858) by Tom Taylor

9 Memorandum. May 13, 1892. 78-3 PNDA

CROOKED PEOPLE

O N A COLD NOVEMBER DAY IN 1895, A QUIET, non-descript man with blue eyes and brown hair stopped by New York's Savoy Hotel to catch up with an old friend. Frank Seaver probably hadn't seen James Creegan since their days together in the Maryland State Penitentiary, where they had both served time for forging checks. It would be a meeting that held great significance, not only for Seaver and his chum, but for Charlie Becker and his band of professional confidence men as well.

Frank Seaver was born on March 14, 1862, the son of George and Mary Seaver, in St. Louis, Missouri, although he sometimes claimed to be originally from Boston. Mary was widowed early and took up teaching to support her young son. Young Frank worked at several jobs, including as a clerk in the offices of the Missouri Pacific Railroad Company, and in St. Louis's Mercantile Library, where he was discharged after a year for "petty theft."[1]

By 1882, Frank presumably felt he had worn out his welcome in St. Louis, and headed for Chicago where on November 22 he was arrested under the name of Louis Figuerado for attempting to pass a $50 counterfeit treasury note at the Sherman House hotel, where he owed a board bill.[2] Later in his life, Seaver did his best to turn the story of that first forgery arrest into one of errant circumstances.

> When I was a small boy a friend of mine gave me a counterfeit fif-ty-dollar bill. It was lying around among his things and I put it in my pocket to carry, just as you would any other curiosity… Some years

---

1   L. Harrigan to WAP, April 11, 1896. Letter. 76-8 PNDA
2   RAP to WAP Mar 13, 1896. Letter. 76-8 PNDA

afterward…I happened to be in Chicago, far away from home, and my hotel bill was in arrears. I had lost my money – no matter how. The clerk became importunate and asked me to pay. I showed him my counterfeit bill. "I will after I get this changed in the morning," said I. The clerk reached out and took it from me, as much by force as anything –he possibly suspected it anyway. He…eventually called in an officer and had me arrested for passing a counterfeit bill.[3]

Convicted of forgery on December 12, he was sentenced to three months in the Chicago House of Corrections and fined $1.00. When he was released "crooked people," he said, were the only ones ready to befriend him. "The only acquaintances I could boast were those I had made in jail…The 'crooks' lent me money and showed me ways to make more and, of course, I was in honor bound to avail myself of their advice in order to repay what they had already lent me."[4]

Seaver's next brush with the law was in Baltimore. On February 6, 1885, he was arrested under the name of Frank Scott for passing forged checks and sentenced to the Maryland Penitentiary for three years.[5] He was discharged on August 5, 1887.[6]

Accounts of Frank Seaver's escapades during the next three years include a lumber selling swindle in New York with a man by the name of Cliff Davis[7] and time spent in prison in Washington D.C. [8] In 1889 he found himself in New York City, where he rented a room at 908 Sixth Avenue from an Emma Van Sickle. Representing himself as working in the cash register business in Brooklyn, Seaver soon began borrowing money from Van Sickle, and showed signs of being an "opium fiend." Eventually, Van Sickle discovered counterfeit

---

3   *San Francisco Examiner*, "Honesty Is Best, But It's Harder." April 19, 1896 77-5 PNDA

4   Ibid.

5   Jacob Fry to RAP, March 20, 1896. Letter. 76-8 PNDA

6   Report. 78-3 PNDA

7   RAP To WAP, March 13, 1896. Letter. 76-8 PNDA

8   Report. 78-4 PNDA

money among Seaver's belongings, which she destroyed. On December 15, 1890, he was arrested along with a confederate, James Tierney, by the U.S. Secret Service for having in their possession counterfeit silver standard dollars. On December 23 he was taken before the court and held on $3,000 bail while awaiting indictment by the Grand Jury, which occurred on January 19, 1891. He was tried and convicted on May 20, and sentenced on the 25th to three years at hard labor in Kings County Penitentiary.[9]

When he was released from Kings County in 1893, he went to live at the Abbotsford Hotel on the corner of 38th Street and 6th Avenue.[10] He opened an office in the Metropolitan Life Building on Madison Avenue in New York, and picked up the lumber selling racket again, calling himself a Lumber and Commission merchant. He continued to have periodic scrapes with the law, and in January 1895 rented an office in Boston as a Merchandise Broker and Exporter under the name of Frederick Stebbins. Boston police became suspicious of him after reports of his unorthodox banking activity and visits from well-known criminals. They picked him up on February 1, but without evidence of anything chargeable, he was released and put on a train back to New York City.[11]

When Seaver went to visit his friend Creegan at the Savoy later that year, he was renewing one of the "honor-bound" relationships that were critical to the combination and re-combination of the underworld mobs and gangs. It was "a hidden universe with informal but complex networks of pickpockets, fences, opium addicts, and confidence men who organized their daily lives around shared illegal behaviors."[12] Most prisons at that time operated on the congregate system, with prisoners being isolated in their individual cells at night, but congregated for convict labor purposes during the day.

---

9   RAP To WAP, March 13, 1896. Letter. 76-8 PNDA

10   Report. 78-4 PNDA

11   *New York Journal*, "He Is Stebbins of Boston." March 16, 1896 77-5 PNDA

12   Gilfoyle, xiii

This was felt by some in law enforcement and prison management to create a "criminal class," When released from prison, former convicts of this new "professional" criminal class usually sought to reestablish those relationships that were fostered in prison, making crime a vocation.[13]

Seaver was the same age as Creegan, and had the same proclivity for the pursuit of great riches in any way possible. Their 1895 meeting was at a critical time for Charlie Becker's gang. With Lenox and English, their two best and most active presenters out of circulation, Becker knew they still needed one more presenter in order to continue their wildly successful run of forgeries. And Creegan and Seaver knew just the right person.

---

13   Ibid., 200

THE ABLEST PROFESSIONAL FORGER IN THE WORLD

J OSEPH MCCOSKER WAS BORN SOMETIME IN 1849, probably in New York, the son of Michael and Mary McCosker, Irish immigrants who arrived in the United States aboard the *Tremont* in 1836.[1] By April of 1864 Mary was living on Varick Street, widowed and the mother of three children, Mathias, Henrietta, and Joseph.[2] But sometime in the 1870s, Joseph took a wrong turn in life, and become connected with a gang of bank sneaks. Bank sneaks worked in pairs, one of them diverting the attention of a teller or bank employee, while the other quickly picked up as much loot as he could, after which the pair would quickly leave the premises. According to the 1886 edition of *Professional Criminals of America*, bank sneak thieves were "all men of education, pleasing address, good personal appearance, and … faultless in their attire. With astonishing coolness these determined fellows commit the most daring thefts. The handful of successful rogues who have attained such exalted rank in the criminal profession despise the thousands of other robbers who live by the commission of small crimes. Aware of their superiority, these men are overbearing when

---

1 New York Passenger Lists, 1820-1891," database with images, FamilySearch (http://bit.ly/2uHDgZL : 15 April 2015), Michael Mc Casker, 1836; citing NARA microfilm publication M237 (Washington, D.C.: National Archives and Records Administration, n.d.); FHL microfilm .

2 Emigrant Savings Bank Records, 1850-1883, Test Books, Microfilm Roll Number:7, Account: 400671860; U.S. Census, New York, New York, population schedule, Ward 8 District 10 (2nd Enum), 180, dwelling 179; digital images, Ancestry.com, http://ancestry.com

chance brings them in contact with thieves of a lower degree... [T]
he bank sneak is not an adept with the pick-lock, but great presence
of mind, a quick eye, and wonderful nerve are the essentials he must
possess to become a success."[3] According to the Pinkerton Detective
Agency, McCosker, as a bank sneak, "had no superior."[4]

In the early 1870s, McCosker, who usually went by the name
of "McCluskey," served a ten year sentence in Ohio for a sneak job
in Toledo.[5] Over the course of the next twenty years, McCluskey
was involved in a variety of failed escapades on both sides of the
Atlantic, often due to his inability to hold his liquor. After a $5,000
robbery from a bank in England, he took his portion, went to "a
fashionable [sic] house of prostitution, showed his money, bought
wine freely and became intoxicated. He told the women he had
obtained the money easily and knew where he could get more."[6]
On another occasion he and several others had plans to rob a county
treasury in Ontario. As one of the men later told it, "It was at the
dinner hour and all the persons in the office except an old man had
gone to lunch. The money was stacked up in large piles in the vault,
the door of which was open. McCluskey engaged the old man in
conversation while [another man] went behind the railing and into
the vault....McCluskey kept looking over the old man's shoulders
and attracted his attention and in looking back of him to see what
attracted McCluskey's attention the old man discovered the thief and
the 'game was spoiled.'"[7]

In 1885, McCluskey was part of an infamous foiled plot to rob
a department of the U.S. Treasury on the occasion of Grover Cleve-
land's first inauguration. He and several other veteran bank sneak
thieves knew that a celebration was to take place and arranged for a
brass band to play. They planned to take advantage of the opportunity

---

3   Byrnes, 7
4   Report. 86-12 PNDA
5   Jan 22, 1896. Report. 78-3 PNDA
6   C.M. Weber to WAP March 25, 1896. Letter. 117-6 PNDA
7   Ibid.

when employees' attention would be diverted by the music to sneak behind the iron grill where the money was kept, and take as much as they could. Unfortunately, McCluskey's weakness for liquor led him the night before the planned robbery to end up in the company of several Pinkerton operatives who were in Washington for the inauguration, to whom he confided about the excitement planned for the next day. The agents purportedly locked McCluskey in his hotel room, and the next day the Pinkerton force was represented in abundance at the ceremony, and the plot foiled.[8]

Finally, though, McCluskey was part of a plot that succeeded. On October 2, 1886, he and two confederates, bank sneaks George Carson and John Burke, were arrested in Baltimore for a sneak robbery committed on the National Metropolitan Bank in Washington, D.C.[9] He was convicted and sentenced to 10 ½ years in the Maryland State Penitentiary in Baltimore, where he met Frank Seaver and James Creegan. When he was released in July 1895, he headed back to New York City, where he had family and a good chance of reconnecting with his new friends from prison. William Pinkerton considered him "one of the most successful and skillful sneaks in the country" before he became so dissipated.[10] And one of his early bank sneak chums later told police that "all the old timers shun him, being afraid he will betray them as well as himself when he is drunk."[11] But Seaver and Creegan were relatively young, and not connected with the old gangs. McCluskey knew that if he wanted to get back in the same line of work, he needed to do it with his new friends. Only 45 years old, McCluskey was 5 feet 7 inches tall, slim with a fair complexion, brown hair and dark blue eyes. With his long straight nose and a distinguished looking black and gray mustache, he was a

---

8   Report. 168-12 PNDA
9   Jan 22, 1896. Report. 78-3 PNDA
10   WAP to George Bangs, January 18, 1896. Letter. 76-8 PNDA
11   C.M. Weber to WAP March 16, 1896. Letter. 117-6 PNDA

perfect type to step in as a presenter with Becker's gang.[12] With the addition of McCluskey, Becker had his new team ready to go.

*   *   *

"IT IS THE policy of the American Bankers Association to wage ceaseless warfare against criminals who depredate against its members either by forgery, burglary or sneak thieving,"[13] read a report of the Pinkerton Agency, by now known as America's national crime fighting system. The Pinkertons' reputation was at an all-time high now. "Seeking out a highly mobile population of criminals was its specialty. The general lack of federal policing and the general incompetence of rural policing left Pinkertons [sic] almost a natural monopoly of national crime fighting."[14] And the most mobile of all those criminals were those who were preying on the banks across the United States and Europe. Because of the actions of the ABA and the Pinkertons, the number of criminals engaging successfully in large-scale forgery had dropped dramatically. By the 1890s, forgers were "a small elite group of little over two dozen...and no one had as great a claim to fame as the forger Charles Becker."[15] Becker was "as cosmopolitan in his habits as he was masterly in his methods," and his coolness in the face of obstacles was legendary.[16] His once dark brown hair had now turned gray, and he was closer to 50 years of age than 40, but Charles Becker was still the man whom William Pinkerton considered "the ablest professional forger in the world."[17] In Agency files of the time, Becker was described as "an expert penman, a first class lithographer, understands engraving and plate printing and is also an expert in the use of chemicals for extracting ink from paper.

---

12   Jan 22, 1896. Report. 78-3 PNDA
13   Report. Undated. 78-1 PNDA
14   Morn, 140
15   Morn, 132-133
16   Frey, 235
17   WAP to John Shore, January 15, 1895. Letter. 182-6 PNDA

The ordinary bank safety paper is no protection against his work…
he is such an adept in his work, that by using a camel's hair brush he
can reproduce the colors so that it would be an exceedingly difficult
matter to discover the alterations in the paper." He and his cohorts
were considered to be capable of doing all kinds of forgeries, and
the Agency warned that "wherever a forgery is perpetrated and the
Agency is called in, it is always well to look to these parties at first."[18]
In fact, as Pinkerton agents were arresting members of the gang one
by one, they were closing the noose on Becker himself. Presciently,
Henry Minster, Superintendent of the Pinkertons' Portland, Oregon
office, wrote to William in 1894, "I don't doubt in the least but what
we will hear of this crowd of forgers on the Pacific slope before long,
as I recently heard that they have been seen in San Francisco."[19]

18   History of the Bowman-Becker-English-Lenox Gang of Forgers.
Report. 76-7 PNDA
19   Henry Minster to WAP, April 9, 1894. Letter. 76-7 PNDA

THE WORK OF AN ARTIST

SUPERINTENDENT MINSTER WAS RIGHT. IN LATE November, 1895, Becker, Creegan, Seaver and McCluskey all made their way to California, Seaver to San Francisco, the others to towns in the surrounding area. In early December, a "smooth-speaking man" registered at the Lick House under the name of A.H. Dean and, the next day, rented office space in San Francisco's Chronicle Building as a merchandise broker, again using the name Dean, where he paid a month's rent in advance. A few days later, the Superintendent of the Chronicle building introduced Dean at the Nevada Bank of San Francisco, where he opened an account with $2,500 and assuring the bank that his account would run from $2,000 to $30,000, and have constant activity.[1] Over the course of the next few days, he deposited and withdrew several sums so as to invite confidence.

On December 9, a Mr. Holmes, who was actually Joseph McCluskey, purchased a draft in the amount of $12 on the Crocker-Woolworth Bank in Woodland, California. This he delivered to Creegan, who turned it over the Becker, who was waiting at Oakland's Galindo Hotel, for his expert forgery. He changed the date of the check, as well as the amount, raising it from $12 to $22,000. On December 17th, Seaver returned to the Nevada Bank, where he deposited the altered $22,000 check. On the 18th, when the check had been cleared, he "presented and was paid in gold his check for $20,000," which was not uncommon if a business owner was paying

---

1   Agency History – Report. 78-1 PNDA

his employees.[2] He left the bank with his four bags of gold, got into a waiting vehicle, and was gone. The swindle was not discovered until the end of the month, when the Crocker-Woolworth Bank gave its monthly statement to its customer, the Woodland Bank, which had drawn no $22,000 draft. The only draft not accounted for was one in the amount of $12, made out to A.H. Holmes.

The banks immediately reported the theft to the ABA, who notified the Pinkerton Agency. The Pinkertons recognized the modus operandi as Becker's. Charlie Becker's forgery skills had by now reached their peak. The expert nature of the San Francisco forgery was described in an issue of the "American Banker" magazine:

> The almost absolute perfection with which the draft had been forged had nearly defied the detection of even the microscope. In the body of the original $12 draft had been the words, "Twelve…..Dollars." the forger, by the use of some chemical preparation, had erased the final letters "lve" from the word "twelve," and had substituted the letters "nty-two," so that in place of the "twelve," is [sic] it appeared in the genuine draft, there was the word "twenty-two" in the forged paper…. In the original $12 draft, the figures "1" and "2" and the character "$" had been punched so that the combination read "$12." The forger had filled in these perforations with paper in such away [sic] that the part filled in looked exactly like the field of the paper. After having filled in the perforations, he had perforated the paper with the combination, "$22,000." …In the places where letters had been erased by the use of chemicals the coloring of the paper had been restored, so that it was well-nigh impossible to detect a variance of the hue. It was the work of an artist, with pen, ink, chemicals, camel's hair brush, water colors, paper pulp and a perforating machine.[3]

"Becker did the pen work and did it to perfection," said William Pinkerton. "The work was so good that when the difference was

---

3   David Carvalho, *Forty Centuries of Ink*, New York: Banks Law Publishing, 1904, 242. http://bit.ly/2vThEwq

found in the books at the end of the month the cashier who wrote the draft had to put it under a magnifying glass before he could detect the fraud."[4] But by the time the theft was reported, Becker, Seaver, McCluskey, and Creegan were long gone. Fortunately, the ABA and the Pinkertons got the word out across their networks to be on the lookout for the men, and their trail was soon picked up in Minnesota.

On February 19th, 1896, a man using the name of D.W. Woods rented a room on Court Block in St. Paul and stated that he was going to get in the wholesale lumber business.[5] On February 21st Woods opened an account at the St. Paul National Bank, which was a member of the ABA, depositing $1,400 and a check in the amount of $1,450 drawn on the Union National Bank in Minneapolis and signed by a J.M. Shaw. The cashier at the St. Paul Bank was suspicious of "Mr. Woods," and called the Union National Bank to see what he could find out about Mr. Shaw. Like Woods, Shaw was a new depositor, about whom nothing was known. On February 24th, the bank telegraphed ABA headquarters: "Two clever bank workers laying scheme here and in Minneapolis. Expect to get about $10,000 from Members' Association. Can you authorize protective branch to nip. Prevention is better than cure."[6] The Pinkertons quickly discovered that "J.M. Shaw" had opened an account on February 19, this one at the Union National Bank of Minneapolis.[7] When they compared the description and handwriting of "D.W. Woods" to those of San Francisco's "A.H. Dean," it was clear that they were "undoubtedly the same party."[8] They also determined by looking at the photographs in the ABA collection that "J.M. Shaw" was bank

4   *Chicago Daily News*, "Is a Prince of Forgers." May 14, 1896. 137-3 PNDA

5   [C.M. Weber] to WAP, Mar 17, 1896. Letter. 76-8 PNDA

6   *American Banker*, "The Recent Capture of Bank Forgers by the American Bankers' Association" [1896], 77-9 PNDA

7   Report. 77-1 PNDA

8   [?] to WAP, Mar 13, 1896. Letter. 76-8 PNDA

sneak thief Joseph McCluskey. The two were presumed to be setting up another swindle like the one in California.

Becker, Creegan and Seaver were staying at the Rhine Hotel in St. Paul, and on February 29, Creegan "happened to look out of his window and saw two men, whom he recognized as Pinkertons, standing across the street."[9] Knowing that they had to move quickly, he and Becker grabbed their things and escaped, while Seaver hurriedly ran to the bank to get his money. But the detectives were waiting for him, and he was arrested when he attempted to close his accounts at the St. Paul National Bank. McCluskey was arrested at the same time in Minneapolis. The detectives immediately notified the San Francisco authorities to send requisition papers, and both men were extradited to San Francisco to be tried for their crime there. Because there was still no hard evidence linking Becker and Creegan to the California job, they were put under "close surveillance" when they slipped out of the St. Paul area and headed back East.[10]

Upon reaching San Francisco, McCluskey and Seaver were held over for trial, while the case against them, and their cohorts, was built by the Pinkertons and local law enforcement led by famed San Francisco lawman, Captain Isaiah Lees. McCluskey was quickly discharged in mid-April for lack of evidence, and followed Becker and Creegan back to the East Coast. Lees had been able to determine that Becker and Creegan were in California during the period of the Nevada Bank forgery by tracking their stays at the Galindo and several other hotels until December 18, 1895, the date that Seaver obtained the $20,000 in gold, when they all, apparently, left together. William Pinkerton, who had been waiting in San Francisco for Seaver and McCluskey to be brought back, did his best to convince Seaver that his friends would desert him, now that he had been captured. Seaver, however, was tight-lipped, so the evidence against

9   William B. Meloney. [n.t.][1902?] 77-9 PNDA

10   [Agency History – Forgers – Becker et al.] 77-1 PNDA

Becker and Creegan was all circumstantial – certainly not enough to arrest them.[11]

When Joe McCluskey finally tracked down Becker and Creegan on the East Coast, he begged them to help Seaver with "fall money" for his defense, which Seaver had been led to expect would happen. Becker, of course, turned down McCluskey's request, and instead proposed that McCluskey travel with them to Europe. On April 30th, McCluskey wrote to Seaver and minced no words:

> Friend Frank –
>
> You are not going to get a dollar fr. These people. I myself am without the means even to look about for you.... I have done my best and failed. If it was not for a disinterested man over here, I could not have had car fare, as I am done and cannot look to borrow money without the prospects of paying back. I do not know how you will take this part, but if these people are going to do to you as I feel satisfied they have done to others, if I was where you are, I would be justified in taking their hellish way of doing business in my own hands and calling them to a halt. I know our way of looking at such things and of the false ideas we have of how others look at them, but you can say that I say this and for 30 years I took all of my medicine without a murmur. This Dutchman has had a life of amusement with people whom he drops like a bad piece of paper when it is no use to him, so I end as I began. I can not even get the money that was given to me for R.R. fare. This is the situation and I tell you to save yourself. I wish Wilson or any of our friends out there to know I am not to be held for what I cannot procure. I have good witnesses who will say I done all I could. Think over this and write a receipt of this to your friend,
>
> Joe[12]

After receiving McCluskey's letter, Seaver knew that William Pinkerton had been correct - Becker and Creegan had no intention of helping him. He wrote back to Joe almost immediately:

---

11 Report. 77-1 PNDA
12 Joe McCluskey to Frank Seaver, April 30, 1896. Letter. 76-8 PNDA

My Dear Joe —

Yours of the 30th is at hand. Coming on top of your last, it has been a complete surprise to me and has knocked the ground from under my feet. I am sure that you have done your best. In the future something may turn up, and you can serve me best by serving my wife. I am disappointed in Jimmie… My case comes up Friday, May 8th and I will take the dose.

　　As ever, Frank[13]

With nothing to lose, Seaver decided to have his revenge on Becker and make a full confession. On May 8, 1896, he testified before the Grand Jury that Becker had raised the check draft $12 to $22,000, that Creegan had been the middleman, and that he, Seaver, had been the presenter. Detective Lees, and the Pinkerton Agency, now had enough to go on, and with Seaver's confession the Grand Jury indicted Becker and Creegan for the Nevada Bank forgery May 8.[14]

On April 18th, the two men had been spotted in Philadelphia by Pinkerton operatives George Butler and Edward Wilson, and picked up by Philadelphia police as "suspicious characters."[15] They were found with steamship tickets in their pockets for passage to Guatemala, as well as $20 gold pieces minted in San Francisco with the date 1895. In addition, Becker was carrying a valise that included:

1. Two bottles containing chemicals
2. One bottle containing white powder
3. One small sharpening stone incased in wood
4. One lot of fine brushes
5. One lot of quill-shaped pens
6. One tin box, full, containing artist's materials, all colors
7. One small knife, point ground to a fine edge

13　Frank Seaver to Joe McCluskey, May 6, 1896. Letter. 76-8 PNDA
14　Untitled Report. Aug 29, 1896. 77-1 PNDA
15　Edward Gaylor to George Bangs, April 27, 1896. Letter. 76-8 PNDA

8. One fine rubber eraser

9. One large magnifying glass

10. One block of hard wood, polished, one inch thick, five by four inches

11. One book containing samples of fine paper

12. A quantity of fine paper, loose, some resembling isinglass[16]

The two were promptly confined in a local police station. A hearing was held on the 23rd, on charges of "conspiracy to swindle a San Francisco bank out of $22,000,"[17] and writs of foreign attachment were served under the Fraudulent Debtors Act. But without enough evidence to indict them, the men were quickly released – after the ship on which they had booked passage had sailed.[18] Once the California indictments came down, however, the Agency had what it needed to arrest both men and set about lying in wait, to capture them together.

---

16 *The American Banker,* "The American Bankers' Association Makes Another Important Capture of Bank Forgers [May 1896?] 77-6 PNDA

17 *Philadelphia Public Ledger,* "From $12 To $22,000." April 23, 1896.

18 [Agency History – Forgers – Becker et al.] 77-1 PNDA

THERE GOES THE BOODLE

WITH SEAVER'S CONFESSION AND THE INFORMA-
tion William Pinkerton obtained from Dick Lenox
during his interview with him on the Milwaukee
train, the Pinkertons felt they had enough to arrest Becker and Creegan. Becker and his wife were still living in Brooklyn, at 78 Bradford
Street, and Creegan was known to be staying at the Park Hotel in
Newark, New Jersey. The detectives knew they had to bring them in
together, or risk one of them getting away.

On May 13, 1896, they finally got their chance. Becker was seen
entering the Park Hotel and shortly afterwards, both men walked
out together, closely followed by Pinkerton operatives and a Newark police detective. At the corner of Broad and Market Streets, the
detectives made their move. Becker, as was his custom, was taken
peacefully, but Creegan put up a fight and attempted, unsuccess-
fully, to escape. When searched, Creegan "was found to have $2,345
on his person, bills of $100, and one for $1000 being found sewed
inside his clothes. On seeing these bills found on his partner, Becker
coolly commented: 'There goes the [boodle].' An affidavit made by
Becker was also found on Creegan, stating that Creegan had nothing
to do with the swindle, and had never had possession of the 'raised'
draft."[1] As soon as word was received in California of the arrest, San
Francisco's Detective Ross Whittaker headed for Sacramento to have
extradition papers signed by California Governor James Budd. Whittaker and Detective John Seymour then jumped on the next train for

---

1 Agency History – Forgers. 77-1 PNDA

New Jersey.[2] "There can be no doubt," said William Pinkerton on May 14, "that in capturing Charles Becker we have secured a man who is by all odds the cleverest forger in the country."[3] And the ABA, in their next issue of *The American Banker*, crowed that "through the detective agency employed by its Protective Committee, [they] succeeded last week in making a capture of Charles Becker and James Cregan [sic], the master spirits of the most dangerous gang of forgers ever known in this country. It was to check the operations of Becker and his associates," they reminded their constituency, "that the protective feature of the American Bankers' Association was first conceived and adopted."[4]

The two men were arraigned before Justice Mott on May 20, represented by former Senator M.T. Barrett, who stated that their defense would simply be that "they were not the men wanted in San Francisco."[5] Neither man made any statement. Detectives Whittaker and Seymour of the San Francisco police department were waiting, and left immediately for San Francisco with the men to face the charges.[6]

The trial of Creegan and Becker began on July 1, 1896. According to observers, "the courtroom was packed with bankers who considered these men to be the most dangerous forgers in the world."[7] On July 6, Joe McCluskey testified that he had "seen and recognized" Becker in on the street in Oakland in December. He testified that he had come to California on November 20th, 1895, "partly on account of his health and partly on some 'little business' which Creegan had proposed, but the details of which [he] knew nothing about.

2   *San Francisco Call*, "The Princes of Forgers," May 15,1896 p.7 http://bit.ly/2vIs4gJ

3   *Chicago Daily News*. "Is a Prince of Forgers." May 14, 1896. 137-3 PNDA

4   *American Banker*, May 20, 1896. 77-5 PNDA

5   Agency History – Forgers. 77-1 PNDA

6   CT, "Noted Bank Swindlers In Town," May 29, 1896

7   William B. Secrest, *Dark and Tangled Threads of Crime* (Sanger, California: World Dancer Press, 2004), 271. http://bit.ly/2i6vabt

On the morning of the 17th," he said," Seaver told [him] that he had received a draft which Becker had raised from $12 to $22,000."[8] He also stated that Creegan had given him a package filled with brushes, acid, inks, pens and tracing paper "to take back to New York." That night, he said, he and Seaver left for New York, where he returned the forgery tools to Creegan, who arrived a few days later. The hotly contested trial lasted ten days, and, despite being vigorously defended by attorneys Peter Dunne and H.T. McPike, "two of the ablest criminal lawyers in California," on Saturday, July 11 the men were found guilty and convicted of forgery.[9] On August 28, after multiple delays, the two were sentenced to life imprisonment in San Quentin State Penitentiary. [10]

Becker and Creegan appealed their conviction to the California Supreme Court on the grounds that Seaver's testimony was not "sufficiently corroborated" and the conviction was reversed.[11] A new trial started on October 26, 1898 after law enforcement felt they had more corroborative testimony to present, including the fact that the forgery tools found on Becker when he was arrested in New Jersey were "identical with a package which was sent to him from [San Francisco], and which he said he threw in the Schuylkill River."[12] William Pinkerton also testified that the men, prior to their arrest, had a habit of paying their bills in $20 gold pieces minted in San Francisco with the date of 1895, corresponding to the coin given to Seaver when he cashed the bogus check. This second trial resulted in a hung jury on November 17, although it was thought that "undue influence" had been used to keep the two men from being convicted. A man who was known to be clever at influencing jurors had been a

---

8   SFC, "McClosker Says He Saw Becker." July 7, 1896 http://bit.ly/2wfCKpq

9   Report. 77-1 PNDA

10   Report, August 29, 1896. 77-1 PNDA

11   *San Francisco Examiner*, "Where Gold Coin is a Curiosity." Nov 3, 1898. 77-6 PNDA

12   Ibid.

constant presence at the trial and three jurors held out for acquittal.[13] Finally, a third trial date was set. At this point, Becker learned that Creegan had agreed to turn state's evidence. Charlie offered to plead guilty if the prosecution would guarantee a sentence of no more than seven years in prison. Finally, on December 9, 1898, Becker was sentenced to seven years imprisonment. A local newspaper reported "the only favor he asked from the court was that he might remain in the County Jail long enough to eat his Christmas dinner with his wife," who was on her way to the west coast after learning of his sentence.[14] The court granted his request, and he was received in San Quentin on December 31.[15] Creegan was re-tried on March 25, 1899 and was sentenced to two years in Folsom Penitentiary.[16] That same day Frank Seaver, whose usefulness as a witness "was terminated," was released from prison on his own recognizance, in consideration of his testimony against Becker and Creegan.[17]

*   *   *

Becker, Creegan, Lenox, and English, along with nearly all the peripheral players in Charles Becker's orbit, were now in prison. Bob Bowman, the stoolpigeon, was hiding in England, far from the possibility of retaliation from his underworld friends. The Pinkertons, and the ABA, were convinced that they had broken up this "most dangerous gang of forgers,"[18] and had put in place the kind of safeguards that would make this style of wholesale forgery obsolete. They were, largely, correct. Improved methods of communication,

---

13   *The American Banker*, "Becker Sentenced," Dec 14, 1898. [77] PNDA

14   SFE, [True wifely devotion...] Dec 25, 1898 77-9 PNDA

15   WAP to John Cornish, Sept 19, 1904. Letter. 76-10 PNDA

16   Agency History – Forgers. 77-1 PNDA

17   *The American Banker*, "Two Years for Cregan – Geer Gets Three Years." April 5, 1899. 86-11 PNDA

18   *The American Banker*, "Becker Sentenced," Dec 14, 1898. [77] PNDA

the new protective features of the ABA, and the nationwide net that the Pinkertons were able to cast, all contributed to the decline of the type of forgery cons at which Becker and his friends were so adept. In fact, within a few years William was able to report that "forgeries have practically been done away with since the formation of the protective branch of the American Bankers' Association." When banks displayed their membership sign prominently, it was "a signal [to forgers] to keep away, and the boys know it, and under no circumstances can you get a professional forger to go up against it."[19]

But the Pinkerton Detective Agency was about more than simply catching criminals. How those "criminals" were treated, especially after they had paid their debt to society, was an important part of the Pinkerton code. From its inception, the Agency was concerned with how the law-breaker was treated at the time of capture, during his trial and imprisonment, and even more important, how he was re-introduced into society and assisted to become a productive and contributing citizen. It was commonplace for the Agency's detectives, especially its principals, to maintain ongoing relationships with these men, and the members of Charlie Becker's gang, in the final chapters of their lives, found that out. Robert and William Pinkerton followed in the footsteps of their father, operating on his principle that "kindness and justice should go hand in hand, whenever it is possible, in the dealings of the Detective with the Criminal. There is no human being so degraded but there is some little bright spark of conscience and of right still existing in him; and, whenever it is possible, the Detective should endeavor to reach this and cultivate it."[20]

19   *Seattle Post*, "William A. Pinkerton Says Professional Crooks of Note are Scarce." Dec 14, 1902. 77-7 PNDA
20   Pinkerton, *Professional Thieves and the Detective*, 14.

PART FOUR

"The supreme assurance of many professional thieves is startling in the extreme. The same grade of talent, bravery and brilliancy of execution in the life of an honest man would make him a great financier, or a great general of armies or commander of multitudes."
   —*Allen Pinkterton,* Professional Thieves and the Detective
      (p.141)

"The detective's trade consists not in pursuing but in forming friendships with criminals."
   —*Lincoln Steffens,* The Autobiography of Lincoln Steffens

A DIFFICULT MAN TO
KEEP BEHIND BARS

ICK LENOX WAS RELEASED FROM THE MILWAUKEE House of Corrections on June 10, 1897, after serving nearly two years for the Milwaukee forgeries. The Pinkerton Agency, in their 1895 report to the ABA, had been clear: "We have to recommend that at the expiration of his two-years sentence in Wisconsin, the American Bankers' Association see to it that Richard Lenox is taken to Iowa to be tried for swindling the Corn Exchange Bank of Sioux City, where there is a good case against him."[1] As early as March 18th, Superintendent Bangs wrote to William Pinkerton in Chicago wondering whether commutation was allowed in the House of Corrections as it was in the Wisconsin State Prison. If so, the Agency calculated Lenox would be released around May 25th. "I suggest," wrote Bangs, "that you inquire into this so there will be no chance of his escaping being taken to Sioux City."[2] Pinkerton responded that the matter had already been taken care of, as "Sheriff Davenport, of Sioux City, was fully advised in regard to 'Big Dick's' discharge in June." But he feared that some Milwaukee authorities were eager to see Lenox go free, and "urged them strongly to do nothing that would interfere with the Sioux City people getting possession of him."[3]

On the 10th, Sheriff Davenport was waiting to re-arrest Lenox for

---

1   Pinkerton's National Detective Agency, Annual Report to American Bankers' Association, 1895, 23. 78-1 PNDA
2   George Bangs to WAP, March 18, 1897. Letter. 76-8 PNDA
3   WAP to George Bangs, Mar 22, 1897. Letter. 76-8 PNDA

swindling the Corn Exchange Bank and the Security National bank in Sioux City, the crimes for which Joe English was already serving a prison sentence of twelve years in the Iowa State Penitentiary at Anamosa, where he had been transferred in November of 1894.[4] The Sheriff got him, but his detention was short-lived. Lenox's new attorney, Jared Thompson, Jr., quickly had him brought before Court Commissioner Hugh Ryan, claiming that the certified copy of the indictment from Iowa was "irregular, because it did not bear the indorsement of the foreman of the grand jury, certifying that it was a true bill."[5] Commissioner Ryan agreed, and Lenox was released to his attorney on a writ of habeas corpus. But the "real reason" Lenox was released, according to Attorney Thompson, was that the ABA had promised Lenox, in light of information he provided that led to the arrest of Becker and Creegan, that he would not be prosecuted for the Iowa crimes on his release from prison in Wisconsin. In contradiction to ABA President Odell's letter to the Wisconsin Governor in 1895, Thompson said that the Banking Association "appreciates its obligations and its duty in the line of public policy, not to prosecute [Lenox] further, and is not doing so. On the contrary, it discountenances this attempted return of Lenox to Iowa in the extradition proceedings....There is a legal obligation upon the public authorities to respect the inducements and promises that were held out to him in consideration of the evidence which he furnished, as much so as though he had turned state's evidence upon a trial..."[6]

Whether the American Banking Association made assurances to Lenox or not, the missing signature on the indictment was enough to secure Lenox's release, and by June 11 he and his attorney had disappeared. The report in the Pinkerton Agency files was brief: "Richard Lenox alias Big Dick, the forger, recently associated with the Becker,

---

4   Tom Davis to H.S. Mosher, May 8, 1941. Letter. 76-11 PNDA

5   *Chicago Chronicle*, "Richard Lenox Goes Free." June 11, 1897. 77-6 PNDA

6   *Milwaukee Sentinel*, "Bankers Gave a Pledge." June 10, 1897. 77-6 PNDA

Cregan band of forgers, was released from prison at Milwaukee, Wis., on June 10th, 1897, and is now at large."[7] He was, as the American Banker magazine reported, "a difficult man to keep behind bars."[8]

Lenox, though, like most of us, was a creature of habit, and the authorities banked on that. Often, when Lenox disappeared, he ended up back in Philadelphia and its environs. When he had escaped capture by the Milwaukee police in 1894 he was found in the seaside town of Absecon, New Jersey, not far from Atlantic City. The Agency made the assumption that he would head back to his comfort zone, and alerted the Philadelphia and Atlantic City authorities that Lenox was again on the loose. Woodbury County, Iowa, Sheriff W. C. Davenport was already in Atlantic City with the warrant for Lenox's arrest. "I learned that he was arrested here two years ago for a similar crime," he said, "and my long acquaintance with criminals has imparted to me the knowledge…that a hardened criminal after he is released from prison in nine cases out of ten drifts back to the town from when he was taken."[9] Sure enough, it wasn't long before he was spotted. He arrived in Atlantic City around June 27th, stopping at the Grand Pacific Hotel, where after several days of being observed by local police, he was finally arrested on July 1, 1897. Local newspaper reports said he had returned to Atlantic City to see his lawyer and pick up a watch that he had left with him at the time of his 1894 arrest. On that Thursday afternoon, one local report said Lenox was "reclining in a chair on the hotel porch," when Atlantic City detectives walked up to him and quickly handcuffed him.[10] Other reports say he was taken in the barroom of the hotel. Once he was arrested, Sheriff Davenport immediately headed to Trenton to pick up requisition papers from New Jersey's Governor John W.

7   Report. [June 1897]. 78-3 PNDA

8   *The American Banker*, "Another Forger Captured." July 7, 1897. 77-6 PNDA

9   ACR, "Old Dick Lennox Caught Napping." July 3, 1897. 77-6 PNDA

10   NYT, "Forger Lennox Again a Prisoner." July 1, 1897. 77-6 PNDA

Griggs.[11] Lenox was held in the local jail to await Davenport's return, and by 10:25 that evening the Sheriff and his prisoner were on their way to Iowa, but not before Lenox shook hands with the Atlantic City police chief, while he "jokingly referred to his former experience at the hands of the local police."[12] "He expressed sorrow," said a local report, "that his seashore vacation had been so unceremoniously [sic] cut short," and that "he had been desirous of spending the summer here."[13] With Lenox's escape record, Davenport made sure that he and Lenox were in a closed stateroom, where he chained his leg irons securely to the steam pipes, not even softening to Dick's pleading to be allowed to walk up and down on the platform before the train left the station.[14]

Sheriff Davenport and his charge arrived back in Sioux City early on Sunday, July 4, where Lenox was lodged in the Woodbury County jail. Interviewed by a reporter from the *Sioux City Times*, Lenox turned on his charm and affability. "Well, you see I am back here'" he said.

> I am sorry I did not come in the first place, for I would much rather be in the penitentiary than be hunted all over the country. But I am an old man, and I want to live a part of my life a free man and I will say right here I am through with all of the old business. If I live to get out of this scrape I will end my days as an honest man should. Another thing I wish to say is that I never authorized the statement in Milwaukee that the Pinkertons had been told to let up on me by the Bankers' association. I suppose that was done by my lawyer to create sympathy for me. Of course I got away at Milwaukee, for will not any man grasp the last straw, especially for his liberty?"[15]

---

11   Ibid.

12   Op.cit. "Old Dick Lennox…."

13   *Atlantic City Press*, "Lennox on the Way to Iowa." July 3, 1897. 77-6 PNDA

14   *Pittsburgh Commercial Gazette*, "Was Chained to the Car." July 3, 1897. 77-6 PNDA

15   SCT, "The Sheriff Brings Him." July 5, 1897. 77-6 PNDA

Lenox had aged since he was last in Sioux City, with his hair nearly white and a short beard making him look a bit different. The reporter went on to describe Lenox as a very pleasant man to talk to. "He uses no profanity and answers every question in a polite manner." Lenox was quite garrulous with his interviewer, and his conversation ranged over his entire life, from his birth in Lancaster County to his many arrests and imprisonments, although some of his "facts" were not strictly true. "That story that has been circulated about me being a desperate man is utter nonsense," he said. "I never harmed a man in my life in a physical way, and just as soon as I see that the officers are armed with the proper papers to take me I am ready to go without making any fight." He claimed not to remember the name of the man who "converted him to a life of crime" in Philadelphia, but he did talk freely about the methods of the Becker gang, telling the reporter that he, Creegan and English "got the drafts and sent them to Becker, who did the fine work in raising them."[16]

On the morning of July 5th, Lenox plead guilty to his crimes against the Corn Exchange Bank, after waiving arraignment and saying that he did not wish the services of an attorney.[17] That evening, he was sentenced to four years in the State Penitentiary in Anamosa. While awaiting his sentencing, Lenox's talkative streak continued when he had the opportunity to talk with the teller David Brownlee, from the Security National Bank, who had actually paid one of his raised drafts. He said to Brownlee that "he hoped he felt like forgiving him for the wrong he had done,"[18] which the teller assured him he had. Lenox then assured Brownlee that this type of "trick" would be nearly impossible in the future. "Pinkerton himself explained to me," he said, "how this bankers association which has been organized since I passed that raised draft on you, has supplied every member with a photograph of each man engaged in the line which has been

---

16   Ibid.

17   SCT, "Admits He Is Guilty." July 5, 1897. 77-6 PNDA

18   SCT, "Sent Up For Four Years." July 6, 1897. 77-6 PNDA

my undoing."[19] He also admitted to Brownlee that he once looked "all over the state of Maryland" to find a bank without the new protective features, but couldn't find even one.

Sheriff Davenport notified the Pinkertons on July 10th that he had transported Lenox to Anamosa on the 6th. "Dick told me to give you his best regards when I saw you again," he said, "and that he was more than pleased with the way he was treated. He thinks he got off in good shape, and will live his time out and many years after."[20]

19　Ibid.
20　W.C. Davenport to Frank Murray, July 10, 1897. Letter. 76-8 PNDA

OUT OF BUSINESS

WITH THE CAPTURE AND RE-ARREST OF RICHARD Lenox for the Sioux City, Iowa forgeries, the Becker-Creegan gang was out of business. Becker, Creegan and Seaver were serving long terms in California, both Lenox and English were in the Anamosa Penitentiary in Iowa, and Bowman, the stool pigeon, was in hiding in England.

Joseph English had not fared well in prison. In a letter to Sheriff Davenport when Dick Lenox was being transported to Anamosa, William Pinkerton said that although Dick would find his friend there, he "doubt[ed] very much whether Joe will know him as the last time I saw him his mind was very rapidly failing."[1] By April 1899, English was desperate for relief. He, or someone on his behalf, wrote to Pinkerton:

> When you were here to see me about two years ago you promised to help me out of here within a year, as I understood you, and as I have not heard from you since, I thought I would write and inform you that my health is very bad and I am growing more feeble every day and do not believe that I can live through the balance of my time in this place. I am almost a total wreck, both physically and mentally, as can be vouched for by the officers of this institution. Now, Mr. Pinkerton, I am, as you know, an old man, can live but a few years at the most, and would like the privilege of dying among my friends and relatives if possible. I therefore appeal to you, as a Christian gentleman, to do what you can to secure for me a suspension of my sentence as soon as possible and by so doing you will secure the everlasting gratitude of myself and family and at the same time

---

1 WAP to W.C. Davenport, July 14, 1897. Letter. 76-8 PNDA

perform an act of Christian charity. Hoping that you will not cast this almost hopeless appeal aside, but at least favor me with a line of encouragement... [2]

There is no evidence to suggest that Pinkerton did anything to secure any amelioration for English, but he was discharged at the end of his term on September 7, 1901. When he left Anamosa, according to the Prison Warden, he was "very feeble, having had a stroke of paralysis."[3] The Waterloo (Iowa) *Times-Tribune* reported on an article in the *Anamosa Prison Press*, which showed the "tender solicitude of the 'pen boys' for an aged convict."[4] The article stated that the "generosity of his fellow prisoners" made it possible for English to make the trip home to Brooklyn and his wife, Nellie, who was living at 22 Wolcott Street. Apparently, the transportation afforded by the state would only take him to Des Moines, where he was convicted. But his situation was so well known that the other prisoners volunteered to donate toward a fund to get him back to New York, and raised $32.00, which assured he could get there.[5]

The article in the *Prison Press* ended with these words: "The old fellow's unlawful career is over now. His remaining days must be anything but roseate, albeit his one friend – she who has remained loyal through all – will cheer his remaining days."[6] In January, 1902, the Pinkerton Agency got word from Pinkerton informant William McDavid (codenamed "Bluestone") that English was a patient in the Long Island College Hospital.[7] He lived through the year, but on December 19, 1902, Joseph English died in the Kings County Alms House. His death certificate said he died of chronic nephritis.[8] He

2   WAP to George Bangs, April 11, 1899. Letter. 76-9 PNDA
3   E.S. Gaylor to John Cornish, Jan 31, 1902. Letter. 76-10 PNDA
4   *Waterloo Times-Tribune*, "Goes Home to Die." Sept 13, 1901.
5   Ibid.
6   Ibid.
7   Charles S. Donnelly. Report. Jan 20, 1902. 78-3 PNDA
8   "New York, New York City Municipal Deaths, 1795-1949," database, FamilySearch (http://bit.ly/2vIcGRD : 20 March 2015), Joseph English,

was buried on December 22 in Kings County Cemetery, also known as "The County Farm." His long-suffering and loyal wife Nellie survived him.

*   *   *

DESPITE HIS PREDICTION that he would "live his time out and many years after," Dick Lenox only survived for two years of his four year sentence. Described as "a fine specimen of manhood" when he arrived at Anamosa,[9] he was still over six feet tall and weighed 210 pounds, although his hair and beard were by now snowy white. His death came unexpectedly on July 21, 1899, with one newspaper speculating that "after more than fifty years of activity, confinement and forced inertia rusted out his vital forces faster than the labor for which he was adapted would have worn them."[10]

Honesty was not one of Lenox's attributes. He had a habit of swearing he would reform every time he was captured. But perhaps the closest he came to the truth was during his conversation with Mr. Brownlee, the bank teller, after his final arrest. "While touring over the country," he said, "it was necessary for me to go to Huron, S.D., and I went by way of Wolsey and had to drive across country about fifteen miles. I took a team, drove it myself, and a windstorm came up, causing me to lose my way. There were no fences nor anything to indicate a highway, and I was very much alarmed for fear I should be compelled to spend the night in a storm on the prairie. The wind took the buffalo robe out of the buggy, and I was left without its shelter. After wandering around for quite a time, I discovered an electric light in the distance, and knew that it was Huron. While lost out there in the country, a feeling came over me that I wished I

---

19 Dec 1902; citing Death, Brooklyn, Kings, New York, United States, New York Municipal Archives, New York; FHL microfilm 1,324,054.

9   *Daily Iowa Capital,* "Big Dick is Dead." July 22, 1899 http://bit.ly/2x4mBk0

10   *St. Paul Dispatch,* "He Died In Prison." July 22, 1899. 77-6 PNDA

was engaged in some more reputable business, but it didn't last long after I got sight of the electric light. I kept right on at work at the trick for which I am now to pay the penalty, and I tell you that one way or another I have already stood a good deal of punishment for my wrong doing."[11]

Richard Lenox's remains were shipped back to his late sister's family in Canton, Illinois, the scene of his 1877 forgery and arrest, where he was buried in Greenwood Cemetery.

11   SCT, "Sent Up For Four Years." July 6, 1897. 77-6 PNDA

DRIVEN TO THE WALL

W HEN BECKER TURNED DOWN JOE MCCLUSKEY'S request to help Frank Seaver after he was captured in California, McCluskey, not surprisingly, chose to forego Becker's invitation to tag along with him as he and Creegan decided what to do next. After writing Seaver and encouraging him to confess, McCluskey also wrote to William Pinkerton to report what he considered was his failure to bring any "satisfactory conclusion" to his errand.[1] He ended his letter by saying that "for myself I am as far as ever from getting a push in life, I know if I got a starter in a little while I could and would be an appreciated man."[2] Signing himself, "Yours with much respect," he listed the address of his brother Mathias McCosker, 35 McDougal Street, where he was living and continued to live for the next several years. Back in New York, with all of his friends either in jail or on the run, McCluskey picked up jobs where he could and spent a lot of time hanging around Drout's saloon on Varick Street.[3] He periodically communicated with both Robert and William Pinkerton, particularly when he was looking for work, although once, when he was instructed by Robert to apply for one particular job, he chose not to do so and told Pinkerton "if I have to seek [work] from those who are not your warm friends I will go without."[4] He always reminded the brothers that "no one in the

---

1   Joe McCluskey to WAP, April 30, 1896. Letter. 76-8 PNDA
2   Ibid.
3   Report. 78-4 PNDA
4   Joe McCluskey to RAP, Oct 11, 1896. Letter. 76-8 PNDA

world has any dearer [wish] for your well fare [sic] than your humble servant Joseph McCosker."[5]

After Becker and Creegan were convicted and sent to prison, largely on Lenox's and Seaver's testimonies, Joe McCluskey no longer had anything useful to contribute to the case that would benefit the Pinkertons. But the brothers remained true to the Agency's code and their own integrity. "A man who may be known as a professional crook or criminal also at times has serious thoughts toward reforming, and I have no doubt the reformation of many of these men could be accomplished if the proper encouragement was held out to them…," said Robert in a Chicago Herald interview.[6] And William, "in a way that was extraordinary for the time," treated the criminals the Agency was tasked to find and punish, as human beings, with admiration and sometimes even affection.[7] So they maintained a relationship with Joe as he struggled to make an honest living for himself, helping to find odd jobs for him when they could, sometimes at New York jockey clubs where they provided guard services, and supplying him with $15.00 a week for living expenses.[8] Keeping him under modest surveillance, they tried to head off his predilection for getting in trouble, and were usually successful.

On May 8, 1898, Joe wrote to William asking if they would "permit him" to move to Chicago. "I can do nothing absolutely nothing to better myself in pocket nor mind in N.Y. And I am afraid that I may break out and do something that will cause my word to be broken."[9] Leaving the letter at the Agency's New York office, he added, "If Mr. William is not in town will you please either forward this or communicate as I would not like to do anything contrary to

5   Joe McCluskey to WAP, Aug 26, 2896. Letter. 76-8 PNDA

6   *Chicago Herald*, "Ex-Convicts and Reform" April 3, 1887. 12-9 PNDA

7   Macintyre, 173

8   RAP to WAP, May 24, 1898. Letter. 86-10 PNDA

9   Joe McCluskey to WAP, May 8, 1898. Letter. 76-9 PNDA

May 3, McCluskey still had not heard anything from Mr. Burns, and was concerned that while waiting, he was running out of money. Saying he "depended too much" on Mr. Burns' word, he wrote to Robert asking for other suggestions he may have for employment though, he wrote, "I want to do nothing you might think was wrong or hasty."[22] Robert suggested that Joe continue to wait for the opportunity with Burns in Far Rockaway, but told him that later in the season, if nothing had turned up, he may be able to do something for him.[23]

By late June, he was dejected, writing to Pinkerton that despite meeting with Mr. Burns and being assured he had work for him, he had never received a word from him. "I am driven to the wall," he wrote, "and being discouraged one day I ran across an old timer who purposed to leave town to do crooked work. I feel ashamed to say so but I partly agreed to do so, for I have no means of living, and never will have in the city. I told my sister I was going away, she partly guessed and said if I had no respect for her to remember my word to you and your past kindness. I have up to date done so."[24]

He apparently was able to stay out of trouble, whether through the good offices of the Pinkertons or small jobs he picked up on his own for the next few months, even proposing at one point that he might join an expedition to the Klondike – Robert responded that he didn't think Joe "would stand that rigorous climate."[25] By the following summer there was a flurry of letters between the Philadelphia and New York Pinkerton offices, regarding Joe's situation. On July 18, 1900 McCluskey stopped at the Philadelphia office where he checked with Superintendent E.S. Gaylor as to whether there was "anything" there for him. He said he had written William Pinkerton a letter requesting help to "pay a bill and get out of Phila.[sic]."[26] Gaylor had, indeed, received instructions from Pinkerton asking the

---

22   Joe McCluskey to RAP, May 3, 1899. Letter. 76-9 PNDA
23   RAP to Joe McCluskey, May 5, 1899. Letter. 76-9 PNDA
24   Joe McCluskey to RAP, [May 1899?]. Letter. 76-9 PNDA
25   RAP to Joe McCluskey, Mar 30, 1900. Letter. 76-10 PNDA
26   E.S. Gaylor to George D. Bangs, July 18, 1900. Letter. 76-10 PNDA

Philadelphia office to get the details of the bill that was owed, and
to advance him no more than $20.00. McCluskey told the agent
that he owed a board bill of $8.00 and a laundry bill of $1.00, and
didn't have a cent left to him. He wanted, he said, to settle the board
and laundry bills, get some dinner, and then go to New York or
Atlantic City, where he hoped to pick up some work. Superintendent Gaynor gave him $12 and reported the entire interchange to
Superintendent Bangs in the New York office, who then passed it
on to William Pinkerton.[27] Pinkerton's response to Bangs reminded
him that if he didn't keep a tight rein on McCluskey, he would be
"about the damnedest nuisance you ever had on your hands....He
can never be trusted in any situation because he is bound to get
drunk every opportunity he gets."[28] His brother Robert also wrote
to Gaylor, instructing him to pay McCluskey "not more that $5 at
a time, and this not oftener than once a week for several weeks."[29]
As he wrote to William, this is "simply an act of charity that we are
doing for [McCluskey] at the present time."[30]

Before the end of the year, McCluskey had drifted back to New
York, and on December 13 he wrote again to Robert Pinkerton. By
now he had reached his lowest point. He complained that he was
constantly being picked up as "a suspicious character," that he had
tried going back to the bottle, which didn't help, and said that "since
the last advance of $5 at your Philadelphia office I have not made
one dollar."[31] Continuing, he wrote that "my only wish is I could
pass away – I am and have been for three months on the verge of
starvation... I came to the conclusion to go to you...as one who has
ever listen[ed] to my appeal – to appeal again in God's name to give
me work at something, no matter how small the salary is, so I can
beyond a doubt convince people I am straight. At a time everyone

---

27   Ibid.
28   WAP to George D. Bangs, July 21, 1900. Letter. 86-10 PNDA
29   RAP to E.S. Gaylor, July 24, 1900. Letter. 86-10 PNDA
30   WAP to RAP, July 26, 1900. Letter. 86-10 PNDA
31   Joe McCluskey to RAP, Dec 13, 1900. Letter. 76-10 PNDA

seems to be in a forgiving and happy state I feel entirely alone in the world."[32]

On December 22, Joe lit a small gas stove in his room. Whether by intent or happenstance, all the burners did not ignite. When he was discovered unconscious, he was taken by ambulance to St. Vincent Hospital where doctors succeeded in reviving him. His brother, Mathias, stopped at the New York Pinkerton office on January 5, 1901, to report the incident and to ask if the agency "could not arrange to have some of the physicians at St. Vincent's give Joe as good attention as possible."[33] William wrote to Robert that Joe was, of course, "an ungrateful little rascal, but I am sorry for his trouble, and anything you see fit to do for him will be satisfactory to me."[34] When a Pinkerton agent stopped at the hospital on January 8, he reported back to Robert the Joe was suffering from blood poisoning and was in very bad shape. "I'm afraid the little fellow is on his last lap," Robert reported to his brother.[35]

On January 16, 1901, Joe passed away. His brother stopped at the agency to notify Robert of Joe's death, and to state that he would "gladly accept any assistance" towards helping with Joe's funeral expenses. Robert authorized a donation of $50, which was gratefully accepted, and his brother expressed gratitude for "the way in which [Robert and William] had talked with Joe during the past few years and kept him from going into a career of stealing again."[36]

Notified by Robert of Joe's death, and the contribution that he made, William responded with satisfaction that the Agency was assisting in Joe's burial. "In the thirty years that I have known him, he has spent twenty in jail, and prison, and while he had me driven

---

32   Ibid.
33   George S. Dougherty to RAP, Jan 5, 1901. Letter. 86-10 PNDA
34   WAP to RAP, Jan 9, 1901. Letter. 86-10 PNDA
35   RAP to WAP, Jan 10, 1901. Letter. 76-10 PNDA
36   RAP to WAP, Jan 17, 1901. Letter. 76-10 PNDA

wild at times by his reckless conduct in San Francisco, still I am sorry that the little fellow is gone."[37]

In a letter to all Pinkerton branch offices on January 22, William Pinkerton reported Joe's death:

> Should anybody at San Francisco, or any point where McCluskey was known, ask any questions regarding his death, you can simply state that McCluskey had been behaving himself ever since his release at San Francisco, and had endeavored to eke out a poor existence... He died...on the 16th, and was buried on the 18th inst. We should not discuss his past life, nor have much to say to anybody in regard to him. Let the dead rest.[38]

---

37   WAP to RAP, Jan 23, 1901. Letter. 86-10 PNDA
38   WAP to E.S. Gaylor, Jan 22, 1901. Letter. 76-10 PNDA

A GRAND OLD RASCAL

Ａfter Frank Seaver's release from prison in San Francisco on March 25, 1899, in recognition of his testimony implicating Becker and Creegan, he made his way to Chicago, showing up at William Pinkerton's office on Monday, April 3. He wanted to ask William whether or not the Pinkertons had been hoping for a longer jail term for him, as Detective Lees had suggested as much to him. William assured him that was not the case, and that they were solely interested in capturing Creegan and putting him in prison. Seaver complained that Lees had not provided the assistance for transportation out of town that he had been promised, but that another man of his acquaintance had paid for his train ticket to Chicago. "He spoke very friendly of the Agency," William wrote to Robert, and hoped that they "would not put any obstacles in his way and if he went back to crooked life, he would not give us any bother if he could help it."[1] Seaver was heading back to New York and his wife Emma, so William paid for Frank's train ticket to New York, "including a sleeper," and give him $10 in cash.[2] "He did not," said William, "expect to receive such kindness at our hands."[3] The kindness of the Pinkertons to Frank continued for at least the next few months, as in August, he wrote to thank Robert for a loan, saying he would "repay this loan as well as the others, just as soon as I possibly can."[4] He included in the letter his card, showing him as a

---

1   WAP to RAP, April 5, 1899. Letter. 76-9 PNDA
2   Ibid.
3   Ibid.
4   Frank Seaver to RAP, Aug 19, 1899. Letter. 76-9 PNDA

salesman for the Ashley Novelty Company on Liberty Street. There are no records showing any further arrests for "crooked" work, and he, Emma and their daughter, Adelaide, continued to live in Manhattan until his death on February 19, 1931.

*   *   *

JAMES CREEGAN, WHO entered Folsom Penitentiary on March 27, 1899, was released after twenty months on November 27, 1900.[5] Sometime during the autumn of 1904, William and Robert Pinkerton were walking in a park in Nice, France when, according to Robert, he "observed a man with a golf cap and knee breeches, who at a distance looked like an English tourist, but on coming closer to him my brother recognized him a Becker's famous 'middleman,' James Creegan." The brothers chatted with Creegan, who told them he was actually living in London, where he was "eking out a precarious existence," and was simply visiting Nice. He assured them that he had "forsaken criminal work."[6] Whether the detectives believed him, or not, they instructed those in the Agency to say nothing to anybody about their having met him.[7]

*   *   *

ONCE BOB BOWMAN was outed as a stool pigeon by William Pinkerton in his 1894 jailhouse meeting with Lenox, "old Bob's" value as an informant went down considerably. When he stayed in England after the gang's 1895 trip, he was trying to put as much distance between him and the members of the gang as possible.

---

5   Ancestry.com. California, Prison and Correctional Records, 1851-1950 [database on-line]. Provo, UT, USA: Ancestry.com Operations, Inc., 2014., 55

6   *Washington Post*, "Police Chiefs Meet," May 23, 1905. http://bit.ly/2fXvkl9

7   Allan Pinkerton (1876-1930) to Seymour Beutler, December 6, 1904. Letter. 76-10 PNDA

Although *Banker's Magazine* in 1896 reported him as a fugitive from justice and that the Pinkertons were "constantly on the lookout for his return," the fact was that the Pinkertons knew exactly where Bowman was. In a letter to his brother on July 3, 1899, Robert said he had "a suspicion that the old fellow is 'stool-pigeoning' for Scotland Yard and has been doing it for a great many years," reminding him that the Agency had introduced Bowman there when he went to London with the Becker gang.[8] Robert had earlier that month received a letter from Bowman, (who was now using variations of his given name, Robert Gillman Stockton) a copy of which he enclosed to William, telling him that he had married, had a family, and had been keeping a public house. Although he assured Pinkerton that he had "left the Becker party some five years ago and have not seen any of them since," he was clearly fishing for information on them.[9] He also wanted to know what had become of the Pinkerton agent in London, so that he could, perhaps, at some time, "do them a favor."[10] When William responded to his brother a few days later, he suggested that Robert put the English police onto Bowman "as hot-footed as possible…"[11] "I have got a thorough dislike for this man," he wrote. "The way that we treated him in the Fritzy Deihn matter and the way he paid us back leaves him one that I have to even up with."[12]

Pinkerton responded to Bowman promptly, but in reporting on the rest of the gang wrote that "your friends, Becker and Cregan, are where they belong, and where they would have been long ago, if you had proved as honest as you should have proved, when all the circumstances were considered."[13] Despite this, he ended his letter by assuring Bowman that "[o]utside of dealing with you justly at

8   RAP to WAP, July 3, 1899. Letter. 76-9 PNDA
9   Bob Bowman to RAP, June 22, 1899. Letter. 76-9 PNDA
10 Ibid.
11 WAP to RAP, July 6, 1899. Letter. 76-9 PNDA
12 Ibid.
13 RAP to Bob Bowman, July 14, 1899. Letter. 76-9 PNDA

times, there has never been any hard feeling against you on my part, excepting for your deceiving us in the manner you did while we were paying you for your service."[14]

At the same time, Pinkerton wrote to Superintendent Donald Swanson of Scotland Yard, filling him in on Bowman, should he come calling. "He is a grand old rascal – exceedingly cute and cunning," wrote Pinkerton. "He might be of some service to you, but don't place too much reliance on him, as he is thoroughly crooked and can never be honest or true to anyone…. He is smarter and a great deal more cunning than he looks."[15]

Bowman had indeed gotten married, to a woman by the name of Hannah Elizabeth Davies in 1895, a woman who was twenty-five years younger than he.[16] He and Hannah and their three children were living at 18 Park Road, Norbiton, Kingston-on-Thames. Bowman continued to correspond with Robert Pinkerton, and in a December 1899 letter again assured him that he had "dropped all bad people."[17] Upset at the "cross" tone of Pinkerton's earlier letter, Bowman wrote "I know I have not done all that was right, but I have not lost all my manhood yet, and when I was hear[sic] in your interest I done my best for you."[18] His wife, he continued, did not know about his "previous character" and he did not want her to know. A Scotland Yard representative did call on him, he reported, but he wasn't able to give him any information about local forgers since he had "lost all track of any crooked people."[19] He closed the letter by asking Pinkerton to "forgive me for my sins in the past and trust me in the future."[20] In an added notation written at the end of the letter

---

14   Ibid.

15   RAP to Donald Swanson, July 11, 1899. Letter. 76-9 PNDA

16   England & Wales, Civil Registration Marriage Index, 1837-1915 [database online]. Provo, UT, USA: Ancestry.com Operations Inc, 2006, 591

17   Bob Bowman to RAP, [Dec. 1899]. Letter. 76-9 PNDA

18   Ibid.

19   Ibid.

20   Ibid.

to his brother Robert speculated that Bowman was paving the way for his return to the States, to which William replied, "I would like fine to get a chance to soak him."[21]

By the beginning of 1901, New York Pinkerton informant "Bluestone" (William McDavid) was receiving regular letters from Bowman, which he dutifully turned over to the Agency. Most of the letters continued the same two themes: wondering what had happened to the other members of the gang, and whether anyone could help him financially, so that he could get back to the States. He wondered whether Creegan gave Becker away, when Becker and Creegan expected to get out of prison, and whether Becker lost his "all his property."[22] He complained in each letter that he didn't understand why his old friends didn't answer his letters, and suggested in every letter that if he only had a little money, he could show them all how to make more with "just a small capital to start with."[23] As Bowman's letters were passed from "Bluestone" to Robert Pinkerton and on to William, the latter was no more kindly disposed to Bowman than before. "Bob is a hard old rascal and I see he is getting ready to go out on the road again. Well if he comes to America I hope he will go where I can get my clutches on him, and if I do, the memory of the past will come back to him good and strong. I would not want anything better than to see him get a dose of about 20 years, and he will get it, if I can go after him. He fooled me once, but he never will again."[24]

In May, 1902, Bowman wrote a long letter to Robert Pinkerton, to report that he had met with a Scotland Yard representative, and to reiterate that he "cut loose from all old associates and…lived on the square."[25] Since he didn't know any "crooked" men in England,

21   Ibid.
22   Bob Bowman to William McDavid, Jan 10, 1901. Letter. 76-10 PNDA
23   Ibid.
24   WAP to RAP, Jan 12, 1901. Letter. 76-10 PNDA
25   Bob Bowman to RAP, May 13, 1902. Letter. 76-10 PNDA

he wasn't able to be of any help to Scotland Yard, he said, and both his public house ventures had failed. "Did any of the gang ever learn I was working for you?" he wrote. "I have reasons to think so."[26] He closed by asking Pinkerton to forget the past and "give a needy man a helping hand that is doing right."[27]

Bowman was still in England in the summer of 1904, and still corresponding regularly with "Bluestone." On July 19, "Bluestone" reported that Bob had told him by letter that he intended to sail from England to the United States on the S.S. *St. Paul*, leaving Southampton July 27.[28] Although William Pinkerton, still carrying a grudge against Bowman, wrote to his brother that "if there is any way in God's world to get him in the penitentiary, I would like to do it,"[29] Robert thought it would be more prudent to leave him alone and keep on top of him through "Bluestone," in case Bowman was "over here on some mischief."[30]

The Agency files are silent on Bowman after this, so perhaps he managed to avoid getting into any mischief. But sometime before 1911, "Old Bob" must have died. The 1911 Census for 23 Piper Road , Kingston on Thames lists Hannah Elizabeth Stockton, widow, living with her cousin and her 5 children – Robert 15, Elsie 13, Dorothy 12, Violet 10, and Charles 6.

---

26 Ibid.
27 Ibid.
28 G.S. Dougherty. Report. July 19, 1904. 76-10 PNDA
29 WAP to RAP, July 21, 1904. Letter. 76-10 PNDA
30 RAP to WAP, July 26, 1904. Letter. 76-10 PNDA

that is so, and they show a disposition to assist me, I shall gratefully accept their help in making a living for myself and wife."[5]

By 1902, Becker's "plan" was being reported in the media. According to one San Quentin official, Becker, upon his release, was to receive a pension of $500 a month from the ABA in return for his promise to "be good."[6] The secretary of the ABA, James Branch, of course refuted the story. "That is one of the most absurd things I have ever heard. Why, if we started in paying the crooks $500 for being good, we would change our name to the Society for the Encouragement of Crime..... We might as well send out a notice to all the crooks: 'Go get a reputation and we'll pay you a good salary.'"[7] He continued by assuring his interviewer that he had heard nothing of any intention to employ Becker, but, he concluded, "he would undoubtedly be a valuable man, and it is entirely possible that the report of his prospective employment may be true."[8] One newspaper even reported that upon his release Becker would be incorporated and syndicated by a "group of New York capitalists."[9]

Whether or not such a plan was in the works, the Pinkerton brothers, following their usual pattern, stayed in touch with Charlie and his wife during his imprisonment. At least once Mrs. Becker visited Robert at his New York office and asked Robert to see if his brother William would visit Charlie on his next trip to the west. Robert related their conversation, saying Anna knew Charlie "would be glad to see you and have a talk with you. She says that it would relieve him to some extent of his imprisonment, to have someone go there that he could talk to." He concluded the letter by reminding William that "there never was any personal feeling between Charley

5 Ibid.

6 *New York World*, "Forger May Get $500 a Month To Be Good." Aug 20, 1902 77-7 PNDA

7 BE, "Bankers Would Employ Charles Becker, Forger." Aug 20, 1902. http://bit.ly/2fL45tn

8 Ibid.

9 NYH, "Raiser of Checks Now a Syndicate," Aug 24, 1902. 77-7 PNDA

[sic] Becker and ourselves. He never did anything against us. It was purely a matter of business as you know, and if we can favor him in any way, I should be pleased to do so."[10]

After seven years of imprisonment, Charles Becker was released from San Quentin on September 28, 1903. He didn't go straight home, but reportedly went north to Olympia, Washington to visit his wife's sister, then headed east by way of Minneapolis and Chicago.[11] The Pinkerton Agency observed his arrival back in Brooklyn in early November, and in December, approached him to find out if he was serious about sharing his expertise on paper and ink making, this time on the right side of the law. Pinkerton Superintendent Seymour Beutler visited Becker at his home on December 9th where he told Anna that his call "was of a friendly nature and for the purpose of assisting her husband." He again assured her that "neither of the Pinkertons had any antipathy against her husband." She responded that she had met both of the Pinkertons, and "that they had always treated her very nicely and that it would be nice if her husband could go over and talk with [Mr. Pinkerton]."[12] Beutler reported that Becker greeted him "very pleasantly." As the conversation continued Charlie questioned Beutler about the fate of some of his old friends like Joe Chapman, whom Beutler thought was dead, and James Creegan, on whom Becker blamed all this recent troubles. He claimed that it was Creegan who "pointed him out" to both Seaver and McCluskey in San Francisco, and that had he "known he had been pointed out, he would certainly not have had anything to do with the forgery."[13] Becker also told Beutler that he had received letters from a St. Louis firm that manufactured checks, stationery, etc., asking him to meet with them about a business arrangement.

On December 12, Becker met with Robert Pinkerton at the Agency's offices where he shared with Pinkerton his correspondence

---

10   RAP to WAP, May 2, 1900. Letter. 76-10 PNDA
11   Seymour Beutler. Report. Dec 9, 1903. 76-10 PNDA
12   Ibid.
13   Ibid.

with the St. Louis firm. Pinkerton offered to connect him with representatives of the ABA for the same purpose, but Becker demurred, saying he'd rather work with the St. Louis company.[14]

The Pinkertons heard nothing more from Becker about the supposed St. Louis offer, but a flurry of letters among the various Pinkerton offices between September 1904 and March 1905 showed that he was still looking to profit from the knowledge he had gained during his career as a forger, particularly in the area of ink. He claimed to have invented an ink that was "absolutely proof against the use of acids on railroad tickets," and was seemingly eager to talk with a representative of the Railway Ticket Protective Bureau. The Agency did its best to help Becker connect with someone from the Bureau, writing to Mr. H. A. Koach, Assistant to the Chairman of the R.T.P.B. (and a former Assistant Superintendent in the Pinkerton Agency) and asking him to meet with Becker the next time he traveled to New York. However, Koach requested that the New York Pinkerton Agency office "secure several samples of this ink" and forward them to him for their own testing, saying that "if the ink proves all that is claimed for it, I am quite sure the [R.T.P.B.] Executive Board will endorse same and will suggest that it be used by the different lines."[15] Becker agreed to prepare several samples for Koach, but at the same time requested that the Pinkerton Agency "procure for him a number of samples of different paper used for railroad tickets on which to present [them]...."[16] Koach said he preferred to have the ink itself and do his own tests.[17]

The Agency had not heard from Becker for several weeks, and when they tried to relay this information to him by telephone in early February, they discovered that he and his wife had left the previous

---

14   RAP. Report. Dec 14, 1903. 76-10 PNDA

15   E.S. Gaylor to John Cornish, Jan 5, 1905. Letter. 76-10 PNDA

16   D.C. Thornhill to Samuel B. Diehl, Jan 12, 1905. Letter. 76-10 PNDA

17   Asher Rossetter to D.C. Thornhill, Jan 12, 1905. Letter. 76-10 PNDA

week for Hot Springs [Arkansas?] due to his wife's illness, for an
indeterminate length of time. Not having the actual ink that Koach
requested, the Agency sent four written samples that Becker had left
with them.[18] When they heard back from Koach, he told them he
had discovered that, prior to going to Hot Springs, Becker had called
on the National Safety Paper Company in New York, where he had
also submitted samples of the ink, which was given a thorough test
with acids and it was found that it did not prove to be safety ink as
far as railroad ticket paper was concerned."[19] Becker promised the
Company that he would make some improvements, but failed to do
so before leaving for Hot Springs. Koach reiterated that he needed
a sample of the ink itself, not writing samples, in order to run his
own tests.[20] Becker finally returned to New York in late March, but
by that time, the R.T.P.B. had endorsed another ink for use in their
industry, and Charlie had lost his opportunity.[21]

Charles Becker spent the remaining years of his life quietly,
reformed at last. The Pinkertons continued to stay in contact with
him. In 1906 they lent him $50 "on account of the sickness of his
wife," and made use of their contacts to help him look for employment.[22] It was said that he won many wagers from friends by forging their signatures "so skillfully that the banks cashed small checks
without question."[23] Pinkerton agents, including both William and
Robert (until his death in 1907), kept tabs on Becker and provided
for him when necessary, including loaning him money on occasion.
Charlie and Anna continued to live in Brooklyn, first on Bradford
Street, where the 1910 census lists his profession as "lithographer,"
and then on Etna Street, where he died on September 9, 1916 from

18   D.C. Thornhill to Asher Rossetter, Feb 6, 1905. Letter. 76-10 PNDA
19   E.S. Gaylor to George D. Bangs, Feb 27, 1905. Letter 76-10 PNDA
20   Ibid.
21   D.C. Thornhill to Asher Rossetter, Mar 28, 1905. Letter. 76-10
PNDA
22   WAP to Seymour Beutler, Sept 28, 1906. Letter. 76-10 PNDA
23   *New York American*, "Charles Becker, Forger Known All Over World,
Dies." Sept 17, 1916. PNDA

complications of diabetes. He was buried in Brooklyn's Evergreen Cemetery where he was joined by Anna who died just a few weeks later on October 12.[24]

On October 18, a memorandum was sent out from the New York Pinkerton office. It listed Becker's name and case file number and said simply, "The above named died at Brooklyn, New York, September 9th, 1916. All offices will remove photograph from galleries."[25] Charlie Becker's run was over.

*   *   *

ON THE MORNING Charlie Becker was released from San Quentin, he was met by a reporter from the *San Francisco Bulletin* who stayed with him on the ferry back to the mainland, and throughout Becker's first sumptuous breakfast in years at San Francisco's Russ House. Maybe it was his first taste of freedom in over four years that made Charlie glib, or maybe he was just happy to have a new audience, but whatever the reason, he spent their time together waxing eloquent on his philosophy of life, his life in particular. He spoke of his work as a "profession." "He is a prince of wits," said the *Examiner's* reporter, "a king of criminals. He has patience, prudence, and ingenuity...Like all successful men he believes in the value of industry. Industry to him is pleasure, for he is an artist in search of the ideal. The ideal to him means a successful job done." Said Charlie,

> This is my ambition - to stand at the head of my profession, to have every police force of civilized countries on the watch for me - and to outwit them.... You'll find ten bold fellows in every million... who dare to step out and do things, who dare to set at defiance all things – including your laws. I am one of them.... I have but one

---

24   New York, New York City Municipal Deaths, 1795-1949," database, FamilySearch (http://bit.ly/2x6NMLG : 20 March 2015), John C. Becker, 09 Sep 1916; citing Death, Brooklyn, Kings, New York, United States, New York Municipal Archives, New York; FHL microfilm 1,324,302.
25   Report. October 18, 1916. 76-10 PNDA

claim to your attention and respect – I am not a hypocrite. How many millionaires are there in this city who would be willing to tell where they got the money? Show me one and I'll show you a fool who inherited it. [26]

"Is he irretrievably bad?" posed the reporter. "How can a man with his corroded heart, his depraved intellect and his sardonic past lead a decent life? He may." Becker looks upon himself," said the reporter, "as far removed from the sphere of the common criminal.... He is an inventor, a designer, an engraver, a chemist, a mathematician, an artist and a mechanic... He might glory in accomplishing respectability, not for the good of it, but for the conquest. He has bested everything else. That is all there is left.....That would be a conquest worth his mettle. Maybe he will try it."[27]

Or maybe it was all much simpler than that. Frank Seaver was once asked about the start of his career in crime, and how he was kept in it. After recalling the many scrapes he was in and the many times he had been caught, he said, "I take things philosophically and suppose I am a sort of fatalist. I'd be all right, I guess, if I hadn't been born crooked."[28]

---

26   SFE, "Charles Becker, Prince of Forgers, Steps Out of Prison a Free Man." Sept 28, 1903. 77-7 PNDA

27   Ibid.

28   William B. Meloney. [n.t.][1902?] 77-9 PNDA

APPENDIX

INDEX

A

American Bankers Association 90-92, 103, 108, 113-114, 125, 128-129, 135, 137-138, 141-142, 167, 169, 186, 189

B

Becker, Anna 3-4, 26, 44, 63, 167-168, 170-171

Becker, Charlie (John Charles) xix-xx, 4-5, 12, 14-18, 20-22, 24, 26-34, 36-40, 43-48, 53, 63-65, 77-78, 85, 90-92, 94-98, 101-104, 106, 108, 110-113, 115-118, 121, 125-138, 142-143, 145, 147, 151-152, 154, 159-161, 163, 165-172, 179, 181

Benack, Daniel 96-98, 100

Bowman, Robert xx, 65-74, 82, 94-97, 99-103, 107, 109-113, 115-117, 126, 137, 147, 160-164, 179, 181

Broadwell, Stephen 96-98, 100, 181

C

Chapman, Joseph 14-18, 20-21, 31, 33-34, 37, 41, 168, 181

LIST OF ILLUSTRATIONS

Charlie Becker – 1870s
> Pinkerton's National Detective Agency Records, Manuscript Division, Library of Congress, Washington, D.C., Container 78, Folder 2

Charles Becker – 1896
> PNDA, Manuscript Division, Library of Congress, Washington, D.C., 183 – 6

Charles Becker – 1899
> California State Archives; Sacramento, California; Secretary of State California State Archives San Quentin Prison Registers

Robert Bowman – 1885
> PNDA, Manuscript Division, Library of Congress, Washington, D.C., 78 – 2

James Creegan – 1899
> California State Archives; Sacramento, California; Secretary of State California State Archives Folsom Prison Registers

Joseph English – 1894
> PNDA, Manuscript Division, Library of Congress, Washington, D.C., 78 – 2

Richard Lenox – 1894
> PNDA, Manuscript Division, Library of Congress, Washington, D.C., 78 – 2

Richard Lenox - 1897
> PNDA, Manuscript Division, Library of Congress, Washington, D.C., 78 – 2

Joseph McCluskey – 1896

> PNDA, Manuscript Division, Library of Congress, Washington, D.C., 78 – 2

Robert Pinkerton – 1899

> Irma and Paul Milstein Division of United States History, Local History and Genealogy, The New York Public Library. "Robert Allan Pinkerton, R.A. & W.A. Pinkerton proprietors" New York Public Library Digital Collections. Accessed August 25, 2017. http://on.nypl.org/2x1kNLN

William A. Pinkerton – 1895

> George Eben Bent Photograph Collection, University of Washington Libraries, Special Collections Division. "William A. Pinkerton, 1895" Portraits Photograph Collection, POR966, Accessed August 25, 2017. http://bit.ly/2gnMl7L

Frank Seaver – 1896

> PNDA, Manuscript Division, Library of Congress, Washington, D.C., 78 – 2

COMMON ALIASES

NAME	ALIAS
Charlie Becker	Bader
(John Charles Becker)	Berrin, James
	Blosh
	Dressel, C.L.
	The Dutchman
	Meredith
	Scratch
Dan Benack	Big Dan
	Johnson, David
	Mason
	Tefford, Frank
	Walworth, William
Bob Bowman	Bowerman, Robert
(Robert G. Stockton)	Collins, Old Bob
	Gillman, R.
	Hale, J.F.
	Hogan, J.C.
	Munroe, George
Steve Broadwell	Man With the Cough
Joseph Chapman	Maguire, Joe
James Creegan	Jones, Henry Gordon
	Quinn
	Quirk
	Woods, O.H.
	Joe Howard
	Russe

PRINCIPAL SOURCES

THE FOLLOWING ABBREVIATIONS are used for the principal archives and monographs cited:

FAP   Pinkerton, Robert A. "Forgery as a profession." *North American Review*, April 1894. Monograph reprinted by MOML Print Edition.

PNDA   Pinkerton's National Detective Agency Records, Manuscript Division, Library of Congress, Washington, D.C., Container no., Folder no.

The following abbreviations are used for the principal newspapers cited:

ACP	Atlantic City Press
ACR	Atlantic City Review
BC	Brooklyn Citizen
BE	Brooklyn Eagle
BECR	Buffalo Evening Courier and Republic
CWR	Canton Weekly Register
CT	Chicago Tribune
MS	Sentinel (Milwaukee, WI)
NYDN	New York Daily News
NYH	New York Herald
NYJ	New York Journal
NYP	New York Post
NYS	New York Sun
NYT	New York Times
NYTR	New York Tribune

NYW	New York World
SFB	San Francisco Bulletin
SFC	San Francisco Call
SFCH	San Francisco Chronicle
SFE	San Francisco Examiner

OTHER NEWSPAPERS CITED

ADB	Auburn Daily Bulletin
AEJ	Albany Evening Journal
ADD	Amsterdam Daily Democrat
BS	Baltimore Sun
CREG	Cedar Rapids Evening Gazette
CRP	Cedar Rapids Times
CC	Chicago Chronicle
CST	Chicago Sun Times
CS	Columbia Spy (Columbia PA)
DH	Daily Huronite (Huron, SD)
DI	Daily Inter Ocean
DIC	Daily Iowa Capital
DT	Davenport Tribune
DDR	Decatur Daily Republican
EA	Evening Auburnian
EN	Evening News (Lincoln, NE)
ER	Evening Register (Hudson, NY)
FWS	Fort Wayne Sentinel
FN	Frederick News (Frederick, MD)
GDN	Galveston Daily News
GZ	Gazette (Stevens Point, WI)
HDR	Hudson Daily Register
IPN	Illustrated Police News
KDL	Kingston Daily Leader
LS	Lowell Sun
MJ	Morning Journal
OCD	Oil City Derrick

PT	Philadelphia Times
PP	Pioneer Press
PDE	Poughkeepsie Daily Eagle
RUA	Rochester Daily Union and Advertiser
SAL	San Antonio Light
SCJ	Sioux City Journal
SCT	Sioux City Times
SPD	St. Paul Dispatch
SH	Saturday Herald (Decatur, IL)
TDH	Tyrone Daily Herald
USG	Utica Sunday Globe
WP	Washington Post
WH	Wichita Herald
WC	Winfield Courier
WDD	Woodland Daily Democrat (Woodland, CA)

BOOKS AND PERIODICALS

American Bankers Association. *Proceedings of the annual convention of the American Bankers Association.* New York: American Bankers Association, vols. 25 – 28.

Asbury, Herbert. *The Gangs of New York: An Informal History of the Underworld.* New York: Vintage (Reprint edition), 2008.

Bankers Magazine and Statistical Register. New York: I.S. Homans, July 1876.

Brady, John Edson. *The Law of Forged and Altered Checks: The Making of the Modern Law.* New York: Brady Publishing Corporation, 1925

Byrnes, Thomas. *Professional Criminals of America.* New York: Cassel & Company, 1886.

Byrnes, Thomas. *Professional Criminals of America.* New York: Chelsea House Publishers, 1969.

Carvalho, David. *Forty Centuries of Ink.* New York: The Banks Law Publishing Company, 1904.

Collins, Paul. *The Murder of the Century: The Gilded Age Crime that Scandalized a City.* New York: Crown Publishers, 2011.

Costello, Augustine. *Our Police Protectors: History of the New York Police.* New York: Chas. F. Roper and Co., 1885.

Dickerman's United States Treasury Counterfeit Detector and Bankers' and Merchants' Journal. New York: Dickerman and Holler, 1896 no. 1.

Drummond, A.L. *True Detective Stories.* New York: G.W. Dillingham, 1908-1909.

Duke, Thomas S. *Celebrated Criminal Cases of America.* San Francisco: James H. Barry Co., 1910.

Express Gazette. Cincinnati: James Barclay: Vol. 2, (January to December 1877).

Fanning, Peter. *Great Crimes of the West.* San Francisco: Ed. Barry Co., 1929

Frey, Jacob. *Reminiscences of Baltimore.* Baltimore: Maryland Book Concern, 1893.

Gilfoyle, Timothy J. *A Pickpocket's Tale: The Underworld of Nineteenth-Century New York.* New York: W.W. Norton & Co., 2006.

Henderson, George Cochran. *Keys to Crookdom.* New York:D. Appleton and Co., 1924

Horan, James D. *Desperate Men: Revelations from the Sealed Pinkerton Files.* Garden City, New York: Doubleday and Co., 1962.

Johnson, David R. *Illegal Tender: Counterfeiting and the Secret Service in Nineteenth-Century America.* Washington: Smithsonian Institution Press, 1995.

Johnson, David R. *Policing the Urban Underworld: The Impact of Crime on the Development of the American Police, 1800-1887.* Philadelphia: Temple University Press, 1979.

The Journal of Prison Discipline and Philanthropy, "Report of the Commemoration of the 100th Anniversary of the Pennsylvania Prison Society." Philadelphia: The Royal Printing Company, no. 26, January 1887.

Lemert, Edwin M., Charles C. Lemert, and Michael F. Winter, eds. *Crime and Deviance: Essays and Innovations of Edwin M. Lemert.* Lanham, Md: Rowman & Littlefield, 2000.

Macintyre, Ben. *The Napoleon of Crime: The Life and Times of Adam Worth, Master Thief.* New York: Farrar Straus Giroux, 1997.

Morn, Frank. *The Eye That Never Sleeps: A History of the Pinkerton National Detective Agency.* Bloomington: Indiana University Press, 1982.

Pinkerton, Allan. *Criminal Reminiscences and Detective Sketches.* New York: G.W. Dillingham, 1878.

Pinkerton, Allan. *Professional Thieves and the Detective: Containing Numerous Detective Sketches Collected from Private Records.* New York: G. W. Dillingham, 1900.

Pinkerton, Willliam A. *Forgery: Paper read at the Annual Convention of the International Association Chiefs of Police.* Washington D.C., May 22, 1905.

Riffenburgh, Beau. *Pinkerton's Great Detective: The Rough-and-Tumble Career of James McParland.* New York: Penguin, 2014.

Rowan, Richard Wilmer. *The Pinkertons: A Detective Dynasty.* Boston: Little Brown and Company, 1931.

Schneider, Wilbert M. *The American Bankers Association: Its Past and Present.* Washington D.C.: Public Affairs Press, 1956.

Secrest, William B. *Dark and Tangled Threads of Crime: San Francisco's Famous Police Detective, Isaiah W. Lees.* Sanger, California: Word Dancer Press, 2004.

Secrest, William B. "A Case of Forgery in Old San Francisco." *True West vol. 23 no. 5 (*May-June 1976): 6-10.

Sullivan, Larry E. *Bandits and Bibles: Convict Literature in Nineteenth-Century America.* New York: Akashic Books, 2003.

Walling, George W. *Recollections of a New York Chief of Police.* New York: Caxton Book Concern, Ltd., 1887.

Whitley, H.C. *In It.* Cambridge: Riverside Press, 1894.

Zacks, Richard. *Island of Vice: Theodore Roosevelt's Doomed Quest to Clean Up Sin-Loving New York.* New York: Doubleday, 2012.

ABOUT THE AUTHOR

KIM Y. WITTEL is a native of Lancaster, Pennsylvania. She has written two previous books, *Wurtenberg to Warwick: the Wittel Family of Lancaster County,* and *Grand Opera in Grand Style: the Lancaster Opera Company Celebrates 50 Years.* She holds bachelor's and master's degrees from the University of Illinois at Urbana-Champaign, and is passionate about researching and recording family and community history. Kim lives with her husband in Lancaster.